ON
ACT AND SCENE DIVISION
IN THE
SHAKSPERE FIRST FOLIO

ON
Act and Scene Division
IN THE
Shakspere First Folio

BY T. W. Baldwin

Mcmlxv

SOUTHERN ILLINOIS UNIVERSITY PRESS

CARBONDALE AND EDWARDSVILLE

In Memoriam

Ronald Brunlees McKerrow

SCHOLAR; GENTLEMAN

CONTENTS

PREFACE

I AM NOT here concerned at all with acts and scenes as such, either as rhetorical or as stage units. In Terentian MS and English plot, the scene is a unit of stage occupancy, as in early English stage plays generally. In the sixteenth century, there was no scenery to change, and consequently no actual place to change, since no actual place was represented. The place, even if any specific place is intended, is frequently a matter of inference. The act was in Terentian criticism a unit of thought, though some critics attempted also to find in it a stage unit. French critics, especially, evolved the doctrine of *liaison,* and embedded it in scenery. The Procrustean scenery was then imported to England at the Reformation to produce various malformations. But with none of this am I here concerned.

I am here concerned only with the act and scene divisions which appear in the First Folio, and what they show us of the kinds of manuscript which lie behind them, in the light of which each play must be considered "bibliographically." But I make no attempt here at such "bibliographical" application.

I have examined Sir Walter Greg's summaries and descriptions of all surviving playhouse manuscripts of the period covered by him for the method or methods of indicating or not act and scene divisions. In print, the period was evolving a system of punctuation for marking acts and scenes in Latin plays —a system which, as eventually evolved, has now long been conventional for English plays. For manuscript, the surviving materials for English drama of the period show that in actual practice almost without exception English dramatists wrote what they called acts, and so marked them. I believe there has been no question that they wrote scenes, which are usually indicated in one way or another. But for the practical uses of the playhouse, the author's own manuscript would be adapted and copied to fit it to the various phases of the play process. General customs were being gradually hardened toward a certain degree of systematic uniformity. The marking of act and scene divisions, or the lack of it, in the quartos (Shakspere's included) and the First Folio corresponds to that of certain types of surviving manuscripts. The present work is, therefore, analytically descriptive of this one phenomenon. Such application as occurs is incidental to the description of this evolving system of punctuation.

Eighteenth-century theory laid the foundations for our present confusion by failing in the first place to distinguish between the acts and scenes themselves and the act and scene divisions by which they were punctuated, whether in print or in presentation on the stage. And the eighteenth-century stage particularly would find it necessary to punctuate, and at times more or less to repunctuate, because of the acquired custom of acting within scenery. The primary confusion here in punctuation is analogous to that in our fundamental system of punctuation inherited from the Greek, where comma, colon, and period referred initially to units of structure, but now for most people designate only the marks of punctuation by which those units are indicated.

In furtherance of the work, the University of Illinois Research Board furnished funds in 1959 for typing the manuscript which, with slight revision, has been used by the press for this printing. Over the years all those responsible in the University have "prosequuted . . . with . . . fauour" my incurable weakness for such research, not only with kindly tolerance, but also with such active assistance as they could reasonably give.

The volume has been put together since I "retired" (under statutory compulsion for age) from the University of Illinois in

1958 to visit at Southern Illinois University. I have made but little change in the manuscript of 1959. For instance, I have kept my references to the late lamented Sir Walter Greg unaltered. I have tried to make clear my fundamental indebtedness to the Herculean labors of that truly great world scholar, and if anyone thinks I have given insufficient credit, for him I have offended unintentionally, and I shall be sorry. When the work of Professor J. Dover Wilson is complete, it will be profitable to check the facts here assembled to his acute observations, by way of application. Fortunately, I have been able to "let in" at the last minute some of the fundamental findings of Hinman.

This volume has been going through the press neck and neck with another at the University of Illinois Press, so that it has not been feasible to cross-reference between them. But the reader will find that each supplements the other.

My own personal library has furnished most of the material used. With perhaps half a dozen exceptions, the Library of Southern Illinois University has supplied the rest. There, particularly, Mr. Alan M. Cohn, Humanities Librarian, has used his excellent training in the period, and his unexcelled ingenuity in the finding of materials, to my great advantage.

Finally, the skilled work of the press in expressing such unkindly materials will speak for itself.

ON
ACT AND SCENE DIVISION
IN THE
SHAKSPERE FIRST FOLIO

Chapter One

THE MARKING OF ACTS AND SCENES

IN PRINTED LATIN DRAMA

THE SUBJECT for discussion is not acts and scenes, but act and scene divisions, and those as they are marked in the First Folio. There is no consideration of what theoretically an act or a scene ideally is, was, or should be, but only of how the sixteenth and early seventeenth centuries indicated such acts and scenes as they had, the application being to the practice in the First Folio. These indications are simply the special system of punctuation which was being devised for plays. The publishers of the First Folio invented no new style book; the dramatists had invented no new "Handbook for Freshman Rhetoric." Both dramatists and printers fitted into an evolving custom, which involved fundamentally total drama, not merely a particular phase in England.

The fundamental system of marking acts and scenes was from the Latin drama, and was evolving through this period, in print. In so far as they had a system at all, this was the system to which English dramatists conformed, more or less, according to knowledge, ability, and desire. Thus in any consideration of the protocol of act and scene divisions, we must remember that the standards in English were set by the Latin plays. The acts and scenes were not numbered in the manuscripts of Terence, Plautus, and Seneca, though the act-divisions of Terence were otherwise indicated by ancient tradition, and in

Seneca by the choruses. The character groupings might indicate the scenes. The earliest printed editions simply followed the manuscripts. "Since Terence was the nucleus of the discussions, we shall find it easiest to approach the problem from that angle of attack. When it came to print, the Renaissance did with the materials at its disposal on Terence exactly what we might expect it to do. The first natural tendency would be simply to put the manuscripts of the plays into print. The manuscripts were in effect divided into scenes, but not into acts. These scenes, however, were not labeled as such. It was the custom in the manuscripts to indicate constantly the grouping of characters. This system involves theoretically a new heading every time the grouping of characters changes. That should mean a new heading, new scene, at every entry of a character or characters, and has sometimes been held to mean a new heading when a character or characters left the stage. There was not, however, then, and there is not yet, complete agreement as to the application of the rule, so that there is some slight divergence in the scene-divisions even of modern editions of Terence.

"The manuscripts, then, were divided into scenes by the massed character groupings for each unit of action; but the units were neither labeled as scenes, nor numbered. Still the critics knew these units as scenes, and referred to them as such. They merely had not invented the modern conventions of scene label, scene numbering, spacing, etc. to distinguish them mechanically. They were at first content with the grouping of characters alone to serve this purely mechanical purpose. The further mechanical distinctions to which we are now accustomed gradually evolved with the art of printing. From our present point of view, therefore, these further mechanical aids to clarity are of but slight importance.

1 T. W. Baldwin, *Shakspere's Five-Act Structure*, pp. 98–99.

2 See, for instance, the bemusements of Iodocus Badius Ascensius on the

"The act-divisions, however, were not indicated in the manuscripts, though they too were known to the critics, and referred to by them. Thus the first printed editions of Terence merely followed the mechanical conventions of the manuscripts of the time, indicating the scenes by grouping the characters of each unit at its beginning, but not indicating the acts. The first step toward further mechanical clarity was to indicate the act-divisions in the printed text. The earliest attempt to do this known to me is in an edition of 1473 by Raphael Regius. The editions I have seen before 1473 print only the text, frequently as prose, and always without act-division or labeled or numbered scene-divisions."[1]

As the scholars of the very end of the fifteenth century and of the early sixteenth gradually discriminated the "correct" form of a Latin play, they eventually managed to get the printers to insert this "correct" form into the text. This form came to demand five numbered acts, which before the middle of the sixteenth century had become fairly standardized for all surviving ancient Latin plays, and was consequently being thrust even upon Latin translations of Greek plays. But ancient tradition did not demand any fixed number of scenes for a play, and besides, the theory of scene-division did not conform to the practice, so that one will find a few variant divisions even in current editions of Latin plays. Strict theory permitted a clear stage only at the end of an act; practice had not always conformed.[2]

Those who observed "correct" form, therefore, whether in Latin or in English, divided and numbered their acts and scenes, and grouped the characters at the scene-headings. For grouping, "The method is, for example, to be found in such Latin plays as *Hymenaeus* and *Fucus Histriomastix,* and in certain English plays on more or less classical lines, such as

point (Baldwin, *Five-Act,* pp. 126 ff.) Incidentally, the French came to obey the rules of their critics, as they evolved them.

Brandon's *Vertuous Octavia* (III. i., IV. i.) and Daniel's *Queen's Arcadia* (II. ii), and in translations such as Gascoigne's *Supposes* (III. i., iv). In all these, characters are listed at the head of scenes though they do not appear until considerably later."[3] Even for the popular stage, one will find a pedant like Jonson doing his best to obey the rules, but ignoramuses like Shakspere and the actors generally marking even their scenes by a clear stage, so that for the stage there was no necessary difference between the act and the scene-divisions. For in their inherited tradition of continuous action there was no necessary difference. With no front curtain and no limiting scenery to shift, they had no more inherent reason to pause at the end of acts than at the end of scenes, and so characters might even "sleepe all the Act," as in *Midsummer-Night's Dream,* the "act" here including the space between acts. If, for any reason, one needed a "long" act-division, that was caused by some local circumstance which called for notation.[4] This practice shows in the manuscripts prepared for stage use in the blotted act and scene numberings to prevent interference with the strengthened acting directions, also in their omission from surviving theatrical plots, etc. The actual divisions may still be there and be important; but the numbering of acts was of little use, the numbering of scenes none, and both might be even an eye-hindering nuisance.

We must remember also that there had been another tradition before the recovery or invention of the Latin one. The old drama of England had been continuous, with units marked, if at all in its staging, by "pageants." Even its thought sequences were determined basically by the nature of its content, not primarily by theatrical considerations. "Pageant" division was mostly a matter of mechanical convenience, thrust willy-nilly into Biblical story. English drama to the middle of the sixteenth

3 R. B. McKerrow, "A Suggestion Regarding Shakespeare's Manuscripts," *RES,* XI (1935) 464, *n.* 2 on *Two Gentlemen* and *Merry Wives.*

century was still in the old tradition. Consequently, if any division was indicated, as in the plays of John Bale, it was analogous to that in sermons, etc. In the second half of the sixteenth century, academic plays, having been written imitatively upon the Latin models would tend to be printed in acts. Some plays from the public theaters might also be so printed.

The public stage as a whole evolved out of the old tradition, with more or less shaping influence from the learned Latin tradition. The tradition of continuous action remained prominent if not predominant until, in spite of the actors, they were forced into scenery—along with females, no less—at the Restoration. The tradition of print for English plays was, of course, eventually toward "correct" form as established for Latin plays. The tradition of the dramatists was in the same direction. By the last fifteen or twenty years of the sixteenth century, it was assumed that any respectable dramatist writing in the current style would write in acts, and the evidence is clear that Shakspere's plays were so written.

4 W. W. Greg, *Dramatic Documents*, p. 295.

Chapter Two

THE MARKING OF ACTS AND SCENES

IN ENGLISH MANUSCRIPTS OF

SHAKSPERE'S TIME

BUT THE PROOF of the pudding is in the eating. To what extent and how did English dramatists indicate acts and scenes? Fortunately, Sir Walter Greg has surveyed the various surviving manuscripts which can be connected with plays for the public stage. These he has classified necessarily and accurately according to their functions. We cannot do better, or even otherwise, than follow his discriminating organization.

When we examine autograph manuscripts which have been used for stage purposes, the results are clear-cut. Among the plays which Sir Walter Greg[1] labels as "Prompt-Books," only "Autograph Plays" are divided into both acts and scenes numbered. For though the copy of *Barnavelt* made by Ralph Crane had both acts and scenes, it is nevertheless only a fair copy by a professional scrivener, evidently from the collaborating authors' manuscript, whether itself foul or fair, for we do not have it to know. But while only "Autograph Plays" among "Prompt-Books" are in numbered acts and scenes, yet the three earliest of the seven autographs do not number their scenes. Mundy's *Kent* does not number scenes, his *More* has neither

---

1 Greg, *Dramatic Documents*, pp. 239- 308.

acts nor scenes and is not really a prompt book, but whatever it had been was being hashed toward becoming one. *Charlemagne,* queried as 1605, does not number scenes, though it distinguishes them. The significance of the fact that these three early manuscript "Prompt-Books" do not show full act and scene division we shall discuss later.[2]

Greg's class B, "Manuscripts of similar Type" to "Prompt-Books" yields similar results. In this classification only Heywood's *Escapes of Jupiter* (*c.* 1625?) is basically autograph, and it is divided specifically into acts only. But, "Though there is no formal division into scenes, a certain distinction is observable."[3] In *The Captives* (1624), however, Heywood had distinguished both acts and scenes. Heywood's own statement on his practice is, "I hold it no necessity to trouble thee with the argument of the story, the matter itself lying so plainly before thee in acts and scenes, without any deviations, or winding incidents."[4] The surviving autograph manuscripts for stage purposes (both classes A and B) would thus indicate that authors habitually handed in their manuscripts divided into acts, though they did not always divide specifically and number their scenes. Even though the number of surviving autographs is small and not as widely distributed as we could wish, yet their unanimity is conclusive, especially when considered on the background of the ideas of the time. As little boys, the dramatists were taught the correct formula for writing plays in acts and scenes, and the record is clear that as men they obeyed to a considerable extent these teachings. Certainly Shakspere wrote in acts and scenes, and there is surely no reason to suppose that he alone of all the dramatists did not mark the acts and usually the scenes.

In contrast, the nonautograph manuscripts among Sir

---

2 See below, pp. 35 ff.
3 Greg, *Dramatic Documents,* p. 319.
4 Thomas Heywood, *Fair Maid,* To the Reader (pr. 1631).
5 The autograph *More* has a note by Tilney forbidding, but no license. The scribal *Barnavelt* has a note by Buck, but no license. Of the six really licensed plays, four are copies, two are autographs. Of the eight which were at least submitted to the licenser, one was undivided, two were in acts, two formally in acts

Walter's "Prompt-Books," except Crane's copy of *Barnavelt,* do not number scenes. But all indicate acts, these indications being inserted in the margin (left), quite briefly. Significantly, Massinger's meticulous act and scene labels in the text of *Believe As Ye List* were cut entirely, but the acts were again indicated briefly in the left margin. For some function in the stage process it was considered necessary to know numbered act divisions for stage, not literary, purposes; but, in this type of manuscript, not those for scenes, and so the stage notations for acts went clearly but inconspicuously into the left margin.

Among these "Prompt-Books," therefore, the distinguishing of both acts and scenes is characteristic of an author; and a mere copy, as Crane's *Barnavelt,* will naturally preserve these features. So when we turn to the nonautographs in this classification, five have acts and scenes, eight have acts only (or with only the first scene labeled), one has neither act nor scene. An interesting feature here is that five of the eight plays which had acts only went into print, but only one was printed of the five which had marked both acts and scenes. In print, all plays from manuscript with acts only preserved the act-divisions, and one of these printed plays added the scene-divisions. The play with both acts and scenes preserved these divisions. Thus for act and scene divisions the plays tend to be printed as they were in surviving manuscripts. And among nonautographs, plays with acts only are the ones which tend to be printed. Probably the chief reason for this is that the licensed copies are likely to be in acts and scenes,[5] and so had to be preserved, only copies, which usually at this period were in acts only, being made available for print.

So far as surviving manuscripts are concerned, it would

and scenes, three in acts with scenes indicated. Thus five out of the eight distinguish scenes formally or informally, as well as acts, two distinguish acts only, one distinguishes neither acts nor scenes. So plays with acts and scenes, numbered or indicated, form the bulk of surviving licensed manuscripts. Such manuscripts would presumably tend to be kept out of print by the necessity of preserving the license.

appear, then, that authors almost always indicated acts and usually scenes, and that some copyists might preserve these features, but that nonautograph copies specifically for stage purposes usually obliterated or omitted from the text the headings for acts and scenes as eye-hindering nuisances, preserving, however, minimal indication of acts in the left margin. We have, therefore, two fundamental classifications of manuscripts that have been used for some functions in the play-house. First, those plays with acts and scenes indicated. These represent in each case the author's manuscript, though they may be only eventual copies from it, and in this respect evidently ought to be faithful copies. Second, those plays with only acts indicated, though frequently in such a way that the indications might very well not appear if the plays went into print. Of autographs, only Mundy's *Kent* belongs technically to this classification, as its scenes are not numbered, and the scenes of *Charlemagne* and Heywood's *Escapes of Jupiter* are indicated but not numbered. Thus a play printed in acts only is not so likely to be based directly on the author's autograph, nor on an unaltered copy of it. Such play-house copies would usually have had some adaptation for the stage.

It is even more significant that Greg's Class C, "Some other Manuscripts of Interest," shows the same characteristics. Several of these manuscripts are by known authors for the public stage, though they show no signs of having been used directly for stage purposes. Two autograph plays by Arthur Wilson, *The Swisser* (1631?) and *The Inconstant Lady* (*c.* 1632?) have acts and scenes. So also have Thomas Middleton's *Witch* (1620–27—scribal), John Fletcher's *Demetrius and Enanthe* (November 27, 1625—scribal), and William Cartwright's *Royal Slave* (1636?). The autograph copy of Middleton's *Game at Chess* is divided into acts only, as are two other

6 Greg, *Dramatic Documents*, p. 1.   *Personnel*, pp. 143 ff.
7 T. W. Baldwin, *Organization and*

copies of the play. But two further copies and the three quartos are in acts and scenes. Robert Wild's *Benefice* (*c*. 1641?) was originally in acts only. Then another hand added scenes "on the foreign method," but the play was printed in 1689 in acts only, not scenes. Again it is clear that at this period authors always indicated their acts and usually their scenes. Unfortunately, all the manuscripts of this classification are probably later than the First Folio.

The surviving theatrical plots also throw considerable light on our problem of acts and scenes, and that early where we most need it. "Theatrical Plots are documents giving the skeleton outline of plays, scene by scene, for use in the theatre, a small group of which has survived from the last twelve years or so of Elizabeth's reign."[6] Perhaps we should emphasize at once the important fact that the surviving theatrical plots are narrowly concentrated in origin as well as in time,[7] so that we cannot be certain that this device was ever used for any of Shakspere's plays, though when Strange's was cooperating with the Admiral's (that is, Alleyn) some contact was at least likely. We shall need, therefore, to be extra cautious with inferences based upon the assumption that there were theatrical plots for any of the plays of Shakspere.

These theatrical plots throw important light upon stage practice in the 'nineties. "According to the custom of the Elizabethan stage, division into scenes is structural and follows directly from the action: a new scene begins whenever the stage is clear and the action is not continuous; whenever, that is, a change of locality is possible. So long, therefore, as the directions are clear, the division into scenes follows automatically and there is the less need for any formal division or numbering in the manuscript."[8] "There is, however, an element of uncertainty here. When one set of characters goes out on the

8 W. W. Greg, *The Shakespeare First Folio*, pp. 142–43.

approach of another set a new scene is usually marked on the
ground that the stage is clear, whereas modern editors continue
the scene on the ground that the action is continuous. On the
other hand, in battle scenes, where combatants are constantly
in and out, old texts seldom trouble to break up the scene: it is
modern editors who are constantly imagining 'Another part of
the Field.' "[9] "In the theatrical 'plot' . . . scenes are basic, since
they determine continuous sections of the action, and they are
always indicated by a line across the column."[10] Conversely, the
author must have written in scenes in the first place or the scenes
could not have been discriminated in the second. But lest we put
too much emphasis upon the units in the theatrical plots as
technically scenes, we should notice that dumb shows, and other
major insertions receive normally exactly the same treatment as
scenes, the corresponding requisite information for them appearing also in its proper sequence between rules. The rules simply
mark off the units of stage occupancy in their sequence, and most
of these units happen to be scenes. But the theatrical plots are
not for the purpose of division at all, though they do incidentally enable us to discriminate the divisions. Nor are they
properly "skeleton outlines" of the plays. Rather, they are for
the purpose of keeping the persons flowing through in their
proper and decent order, and in no way calculated to give the
outline, even though we can infer very roughly the run of the
play.

Further, Sir Walter's strictures on the haziness of discrimination for scenes serve to point up his own overemphasis.
The sixteenth century actually shifted characters; it did not in
any modern sense actually shift either "scenery" or "place." In
the theatrical plots, there may be an occasional "on the walls"
or "above" to distinguish from those below, or "in his tent,"
"behind the Curtaines," etc., all for stage locations; but if a

9 Greg, *First Folio*, p. 142, n. 2.

true shift of scene is anywhere indicated in these theatrical plots I have failed to notice it. The dramatist himself is more likely in his text to ask for such shifts in imagination simply because they could not actually be represented. To those who constructed the surviving theatrical plots, shifts of scene as such were simply none of their business; their whole aim was to keep the characters shifting through the correct stage locations. Later emphasis upon scene as such was the natural consequence of emphasis upon scenery in the latter part of the seventeenth century and following. So far as stage purposes are concerned, the shift of scene in a sixteenth-century play is usually our inference from the actual shift of characters. To leave the shifting characters out of our definition of scene for the sixteenth century is to leave Hamlet out of *Hamlet*. Shift of scene and shift of characters are, of course, basically connected; but in actual sixteenth-century stage practice it was the shift of characters which led the way. Behold the theatrical plots! And the quite hazy scene indications generally, simply because actually scenes were neither set nor shifted.

As Sir Walter's analysis makes sufficiently clear, the scene in sixteenth-century English practice is essentially the Terentian scene. In the manuscripts, and consequently in the editions of Terence, a scene was a unit of occupancy upon the stage, marked by grouping at the head all the characters who were to appear in a particular unit. When the characters changed by addition or by subtraction the scene changed, marked by the consequent new grouping of characters. Scene in the sense of scenery or setting had nothing to do with the matter. A scene was simply a unit of stage-scene ($\sigma\kappa\eta\nu\dot{\eta}$) occupancy. The theorists wished that the characters should shift from grouping to grouping, scene to scene, so that the stage would be continuously occupied to the end of the act, when the stage would become clear. But the failure of Terence to observe this practice uni-

10 Greg, *First Folio*, p. 143, n. 1.

formly caused the critics a great deal of anguish, and few
English dramatists made any attempt to observe this principle,
though the French eventually did. Instead, with the English,
every scene ended with a clear stage, and meanwhile characters
entered or went out as exigencies demanded. Early pageant
practice may have been at the bottom of this. But, at any rate,
neither in printed Terence nor in sixteenth-century English
practice on the public stage did scenes as such have any connection with scenery or setting. Much less did acts.

But for Pope and his successor-followers acts and scenes
were very much beswaddled with scenery and setting, and they
protested accordingly. Those who prefer more or less continuous action, apparently the majority at present, commend
them. But even if their instincts should prove to be acceptable,
their history was poor and calls for narrow examination. Unfortunately, scenes became entangled with the scene or setting
for these earlier critics of Shakspere, who were besides more
interested in dogmatic literary criticism than in historical fact.
And this confused definition of scene forced a cognate definition
upon act.

Apparently it was Pope who started the tradition that the
act and scene divisions of the First Folio are dramatically
absurd—as, of course they may be. "The Plays not having been
before [in the quartos] so much as distinguish'd by *Acts* and
Scenes, they are in this edition [F1] divided according as
they play'd them; often where there is no pause in the action, or
where they thought fit to make a breach in it, for the sake of
Musick, Masques, or Monsters."[11] Pope had thus initiated this
idea of break "where there is no pause in the action."

Pope's idea appealed to Dr. Johnson, who had excogitated
an ideal act-division (not division into acts) for the scenic stage
of his day, in terms of the current theory of the "natural and
proper," or "Nature methodiz'd." On Saturday, September 14,

---

11 A. Pope, *Shakespear* (1725), I, xviii.

1751, Dr. Johnson indicated his fundamental position when he wrote of acts in general (*Rambler,* No. 156,18): "By what Accident the Number of Acts was limited to five, I know not that any Author has informed us, but certainly it is not determined by any necessity arising either from the Nature of Action or the Propriety of Exhibition. An Act is only the Representation of such a Part of the Business of the Play as proceeds in an unbroken Tenor without any intermediate Pause. Nothing is more evident than that of every real, and, by Consequence, of every dramatick Action, the Intervals may be more or fewer than five; and indeed the Rule is upon the *English* Stage, every Day broken in Effect, without any other Mischief than that which arises from an absurd Endeavour to observe it in Appearance. For whenever the Scene is shifted the Act ceases, since some Time is necessarily supposed to elapse while the Personages of the Drama change their Place."

Thinking within the framework of the scene-shifting stage of his day, Dr. Johnson is defining in terms of "intermediate Pause," as Pope had done, or act-division, not in terms of acts. Consequently, his *Dictionary* of 1755 defines an act as "A part of a play, during which the action proceeds without interruption." Further, Dr. Johnson challenges the idea that there must necessarily be four such pauses, marking five divisions. The number of the pauses should be determined by the action itself. Thus on the question of pauses or act-divisions Dr. Johnson disagrees fundamentally with the stage-practice of his day.

Naturally, therefore, in his *Shakespeare* of 1765 Dr. Johnson objected to the inherited acts and resultant pauses or act-divisions on the stage, since they too did not conform to the ideal system he had inferred theoretically as "natural and proper." For, of course, Shakspere, Nature's child, must have observed the natural and proper, and the actors must have thrust into his work these breaks "where there is no pause in

the action" as Pope had accused them of doing. "I have preserved the common distribution of the plays into acts, though
I believe it to be in almost all the plays void of authority. Some
of those which are divided in the later editions have no division
in the first folio, and some that are divided in the folio have
no division in the preceding copies. The settled mode of the
theatre requires four intervals in the play, but few, if any, of
our authour's compositions can be properly distributed in that
manner. An act is so much of the drama as passes without
intervention of time or change of place. A pause makes a new
act. In every real, and therefore in every imitative action, the
intervals may be more or fewer, the restriction of five acts
being accidental and arbitrary. This *Shakespeare* knew, and
this he practised; his plays were written, and at first printed in
one unbroken continuity, and ought now to be exhibited with
short pauses, interposed as often as the scene is changed, or
any considerable time is required to pass. This method would
at once quell a thousand absurdities."[12]

Quite correctly, Dr. Johnson insists that Shakspere's plays
do not exhibit the clear-cut, pausing, scene-shifting act-divisions
of the eighteenth century, and infers that consequently a play of
Shakspere's should not thus be torn apart by four pauses or act-
divisions—though he would permit any requisite number of
pauses for scenes. Dr. Johnson's conclusion is, of course, a
matter of opinion. But Dr. Johnson bolsters his opinion with
Pope's assumption that the quartos represent Shakspere's own
intentions, and the Folio the interference of the actors. If, however, Pope and Dr. Johnson are to use the quartos as an argument for no acts they must equally use them as an argument for
no scenes for the quartos indicate no more scenes than they do
acts. According to this line of reasoning the quartos would
indicate that there were no pauses at all in the action of the
play; that is, that on the stage Shakspere's plays observed

12 S. Johnson, *Shakespeare* (1765), I, [E1]ʳ.

neither acts nor scenes. If so, the practice was not confined to Shakspere, but is found in the heavy majority of the quartos of the period. Yet the quartos for the public stage which were printed in acts, or acts and scenes, are not different in their structure, nor usually in their authorship from those which were printed without acts and scenes. That is, even if the undivided quartos should indicate that no considerable act and scene pauses were to be observed upon the stage, they still present no argument that the plays were not written in acts and scenes. We still need to determine in other ways both the theory of acts and the practice of pauses or act-divisions upon the stage in the sixteenth century.

And we might as well notice here that the earliest critics upon Terence did not define acts in terms of pauses or act-divisions upon the stage, but in terms of stages of the intrigue. Donatus says on *Hecyra,* "Varro teaches that neither in this play nor in the others is it to be wondered at that the acts may be unequal in number of scenes and pages, since this distribution is determined by the proper division of the intrigue, not by the number of verses, not only with the Latins, but even with the Greeks themselves."[13]

Returning to Pope and Johnson, we should notice that they were mostly mistaken in their diagnosis of the cause of their distress. Acts and scenes in English plays were not initially for the purpose of making breaks in the action for "Musick, Masques, or Monsters," or for any other stage purpose. They are a literary structural device, and do not break the continuity of a play any more than chapters and paragraphs break the continuity of certain other forms, but to one who understands their significance are an aid in following the continuity. They are for purposes of exposition (thought), not of narration (action). A play must have a literary structure, just as a sonnet must. And it is very difficult to get the smile of the Cheshire cat with-

13 Baldwin, *Five-Act,* p. 28.

out considerable suggestion of the cat. But thrusting these rhetorical divisions into emphasized scenic compartments upon the stage, as was done in Dr. Johnson's day, did interrupt the continuity. In Shakspere's own day, and particularly in his own plays, despite Pope's alliterative assumptions, there was apparently no excessive interruption of continuity on the public stage, and there need not have been any. It was the private stage which fostered interruptions by music, dumb-shows, etc., and finally forced the public stage into similar habits till eventually it became a private stage. Dr. Johnson may have been flogging properly, but the wrong horse. The trouble was not that the plays were written in acts and scenes, and marked accordingly; but that these divisions had become the excuse for what Dr. Johnson evidently considered to be an excessive amount of retarding matter on the stage.

Within three years, Dr. Johnson's theoretical definition of act was to do duty much more appropriately for an actual definition of scene. Capell in 1768 "pick'd out" a rule of division from a study of the seventeen, as he counted, plays of Shakspere in acts and scenes, "which rule might easily have been discover'd before, had but any the least pains been bestow'd upon it; and certainly it was very well worth it, since neither can the representation be manag'd, nor the order and thread of the fable be properly conceiv'd by the reader, 'till this article is adjusted. The plays that are come down to us divided, must be look'd upon as of the Author's own settling; and in them, with regard to acts, we find him following establish'd precepts, or, rather, conforming himself to the practice of some other dramatick writers of his time; for they, it is likely, and Nature, were the books he was best acquainted with: His scene divisions he certainly did not fetch from writers upon the drama; for, in

14 E. Capell, *Shakespeare* [1768], I, 25. Like Johnson, Capell was also using the critical lingo of the age, "Na- ture" equaling "Nature of Action," and "practice of some other dramat-

them, he observes a method in which perhaps he is singular, and he is invariable in the use of it: with him, a change of scene implies generally a change of place, though not always; but always an entire evacuation of it, and a succession of new persons: that *liaison* of the scenes, which JONSON seems to have attempted, and upon which the *French* stage prides itself, he does not appear to have had any idea of."[14]

Steevens in his edition of Johnson then, without acknowledgement, neatened up Capell, founding the case for Shakspere's own practice more strongly. "The scenery, throughout all the plays, is regulated in conformity to a rule, which the poet, by his general practice, seems to have proposed to himself. Several of his pieces are come down to us, divided into scenes as well as acts. These divisions were probably his own, as they are made on settled principles, which would hardly have been the case, had the task been executed by the players. A change of scene, with Shakespeare, most commonly implies a change of place, but always, an entire evacuation of the stage. The custom of distinguishing every entrance or exit by a fresh scene, was adopted, perhaps very idly, from the French theatre."[15] The French were, of course, following the rules of correctness, which mostly the French critics had promulgated in the name of the classics, and against some of which Dr. Johnson in the quotation above thought he was rebelling. Basing upon the actual practice in Shakspere's plays, Capell finds that "a change of scene implies generally a change of place, though not always; but always an entire evacuation of it," and Steevens accepts Capell's definition, making the further point that the acts and scenes could hardly be insertions by the actors, as Pope had supposed. If any insist upon following the errors of Dr. Johnson here, it is not the fault of Capell, Steevens, Malone, etc. Dr. Johnson had assumed the "French," as they called it, or "foreign," as Sir

ick writers of his time" corresponding to "Propriety of Exhibition." 15 S. Johnson and G. Steevens, *Shakespeare* (1773), I, E3^v–E4^r.

Walter Greg labels it, method of stage structure for acts, had then applied his own theory of the "natural and proper" to get his definition of an act, and had finally bolstered the whole with Pope's argument from undivided quartos. His resultant definition actually applied to English scenes, not to acts as such.

When Capell demonstrated the system of structure for scenes, Steevens and other contemporaries agreed at once that scenes were a matter of original structure in Shakspere, as in effect does Sir Walter Greg. The eighteenth-century scholars then troubled no further about the inherited act-system, in which the scenes were grouped. Rowe had long before divided into acts the partially divided and the undivided plays of the First Folio as they now appear in the Globe edition, except that he did not divide 2 Henry VI at all, and that in 1 Henry VI, Timon, and Antony and Cleopatra he placed the beginning of Act V earlier than it is now in the Globe by what he regarded as one scene, and the Globe regards in two out of three instances as no scene break. While Pope was contemptuous of even the act and scene markings found in the folios, which he ascribed to inter-polation by the actors, nevertheless he divided 2 Henry VI into acts, and changed Rowe's marking of Act V in Antony and Cleopatra to the place now marked in the Globe. Capell then altered the position of Act V in 1 Henry VI and Timon as now found in the Globe.

Thus for the partially divided and the undivided plays of the First Folio, the standard act-divisions in the Globe are those of Rowe, corrected in two instances by Pope, and in two by Capell, who was in one instance following a suggestion by Johnson. It would probably not have occurred to a practicing dramatist like Rowe that plays could be written without acts. Dryden, for instance, had given a version of the five-act formula, which was still in the school texts, attributing it to Aristotle himself, and other contemporaries regularly paid their respects to the formula, as had been done universally for more than a century. Rowe particularly, through Betterton and others, may have known the acting tradition besides—in so far as it had preserved these matters. Even prompt on print for the seventeenth century is likely to indicate act-divisions in some form, as a forthcoming work of my colleague, Professor G. B. Evans, will show. Both from still current theory and from the acting tradition, Rowe would know the old system, which the new French tradition for the scenic stage had not yet in England completely supplanted.

It is significant that all three of the eighteenth-century corrections upon Rowe are for the fifth act, and were fundamentally corrections of the same thing. In the case of *Timon,* "Johnson calls attention to the impropriety of placing the entry of the Banditti in one act and that of the Poet and Painter in another, when the latter were mentioned as within view when Apemantus parted from Timon. 'It might be suspected,' he says, 'that some scenes are transposed, for all these difficulties would be removed by introducing the Poet and Painter first, and the thieves in this place. Yet I am afraid the scenes must keep their present order, for the Painter alludes to the Thieves, when he says, *he likewise enriched poor straggling soldiers with great quantity'.*"[16] As the discoverer of the true principle of scene-division in Shakspere, the clear stage, Capell was evidently impressed, and made the suggested change. This situation had not troubled Rowe any more than it would have troubled the original dramatist, for the stage itself was actually clear. The trouble arises only when these scenes are to be pried apart by an act-pause and curtain, suspending animation as it were. Similarly, in *Antony and Cleopatra* Rowe placed Act IV, Scene 15 of the Globe numbering in the fifth act, evidently regarding Antony's death as part of the catastrophe in accord with the five-act formula, particularly since Antony's wounding

16 W. A. Wright, *Shakespeare* (1892), VII, 136.

of himself in IV, 14 was the occasion of both his own catastrophe and that of Cleopatra. And, according to formula, the occasion of the catastrophe must come at the end of the fourth act. Rowe's division by pulling Antony's death to the fourth act thus left the whole catastrophe to Cleopatra and made Antony's death only the occasion of it. Pope, on the other hand, was evidently trying to preserve the liaison between the two Antony scenes, as Johnson and Capell were those in *Timon*. According to the five-act formula, Rowe was unquestionably right in *Antony*, and may have been in *Timon*. At any rate, he was the earliest authority in the field, and the reasoning by means of which he has been reversed in these instances did not apply to Shakspere's stage, but to that of the eighteenth century. In the case of *1 Henry VI*, Rowe was following the correction of the Second Folio, 1632, concurred in by the third and fourth, and thence inherited by Rowe. Elsewhere,[17] I have examined the evidence to the conclusion that the Second Folio was, according to the principles of Shakspere's day, unquestionably correct in its marking.

In all three instances, we have that hazy demarcation of scenes which, as we have seen, arouses some show of warmth even in Sir Walter Greg. But there is nothing we can do about that now except to recognize it and let it alone—as in principle at least Sir Walter evidently would wish "modern editors" to do. At the time of the Second Folio, the old dramaturgy still prevailed, and as a practicing dramatist even Rowe was still closely enough in touch with the old principles and the five-act formula to follow the original structure without being troubled too much by the new staging. We may be sure that Westminster School, with its already long tradition of acting the Latin drama, would have seen to it that Rowe had a practicable grasp

17 T. W. Baldwin, *On the Literary Genetics of Shakspere's Plays, 1592–1594*, pp. 353-4.

18 Just as in 1914–15 I deduced the five-act formula essentially from Massinger's practice some fifteen years before I came upon the first statement of it (autumn of 1930).

on the fundamental system. French frills would not have penetrated there.

After all, these plays of Shakspere do fall into five literary units each, and for the majority of the plays these units were indicated in the First Folio. Such units as are discriminated there are in the critical works of the day called acts, are in accordance with the prescriptions for acts, and accordingly labeled as acts. Capell, Steevens, and their contemporaries saw that the actors could not have divided so consistently or at all into acts and scenes, if acts and scenes had not already been there. Nor did they find any particular difficulty in themselves discriminating on the same deducible principles the acts and scenes for the few plays which had there been undivided into acts. And this latter group did it pragmatically without any stated reference to the five-act formula, if they knew it.[18] Whoever marked them and whatever they were called, these units themselves go back to original construction, as actualities. The plays are certainly constructed in units, which contemporaries called acts. How the divisions between these units were discriminated, and whether these divisions were observed upon the stage are totally different matters.

Nor should it be overlooked that Capell points out correctly that the change of place is "implied" generally, not stated. In other words, the shift of characters is direct, the shift of scene merely a consequent inference.[19] Sir Walter Greg knows that Shakspere's practice in scenes was not peculiar to his day, as Capell, with inherited critical predisposition from "dramatick writers"; that is, from French criticism and practice, simply assumed it was, even though occasionally Sir Walter finds instances of the "foreign method"—quite correctly, of course. Whether the author himself discriminated the scenes by num-

See my edition of Massinger's *Duke of Milan* (1918), also *Comedy of Errors* (1928).

19 The editors of Capell's day were struggling to get satisfactory "scenes" for Shakspere's plays—editors still are for that matter.

bering, heading, centered entrances, etc. is of no real importance. According to Sir Walter, scenes are organic and functional for the Elizabethan stage, not merely external and mechanical. I take it, therefore, it is agreed that Shakspere, like everybody else, wrote in scenes, whether or however he marked them, or wished them to be observed.

In contrast to scenes, which for the stage he considers to be organic and functional, Sir Walter says, "The division into acts is merely conventional. An author may write without any such division in mind: if he intends a division, and wishes it to be in any way recognized on the stage, it is essential that he should indicate it in his manuscript."[20] "Act-division is not usually recognized in the 'plots.' In *The Dead Man's Fortune* (*c.* 1590) there are rows of crosses on four of the scene-lines, and since in each case there is a note of 'Musique' in the margin, they presumably indicate a division into acts. The plots of *2 The Seven Deadly Sins* (*c.* 1590), *The Battle of Alcazar* (1598–9?), and *1 Tamar Cam* (1602) have appearances of dumb-shows, a presenter, or a chorus that show a five-act structure in each, but there is no formal division. Acts II and IV only are marked in the quarto of *The Battle of Alcazar, 1594.*"[21]

As to acts, I suppose it is true theoretically that "An author may write without any such division in mind"; and if we add "on the stage," as I believe Sir Walter intended, the possibility becomes more thinkable. For whatever be true of acts as stage units, from the view of rhetorical construction, acts, not scenes, are the units which are organic and functional in Shakspere's day. As a matter of fact, it is clear that in several notorious instances, edited out of modern editions, Shakspere did not trouble about the fact that his stage would not be clear at the literary act-division. It simply was not important to clear the stage at those act-divisions; that is, there was no compelling

20 Greg, *First Folio*, p. 143.
21 Greg, *First Folio*, p. 143, *n* 2.

22 Baldwin, *Organization and Personnel*, p. 145

reason to observe those act-divisions on his stage. But this fact still has no bearing on the question of whether Shakspere did write in acts and scenes, and whether having written he numbered them.

While Sir Walter says the "Act-division is not usually recognized in the 'plots,'" yet he lists four plots which have characteristics "that show a five-act structure in each" and the total number of plots is only seven. For the eighth in Sir Walter's collection, *England's Joy,* is not a manuscript plot; in fact, is not a plot of this type at all.[22] For the remaining three of the seven, the third, *Frederick and Basilea,* has "no division into acts" (p. 123), but at one place there might have been "an act interval of which the Plot takes no cognizance" (p. 127). The fourth, *2 Fortune's Tennis,* "is a mere fragment" (p. 130), but at one place "A very tempting explanation is that the words were 'Enter Chorus' and that they marked the end of an act" (p. 137). For the fifth, *Troilus and Cressida,* "a single large fragment is all that remains," and "There is no indication whatever of any division into acts, either in the Plot or the play itself [what play?], and sufficient remains to make it very improbable that any formal division existed" (p. 139). But for all the fully justified emphasis, the play was paid for by acts.[23] So in four out of seven cases plots do in one way or another recognize acts, and there are inconclusive hints in two other cases that acts may be involved, while the third was paid for by acts. We must thus agree with Sir Walter that the majority of the parent plays were in acts, and all probably were, even though their plots were not specifically divided.

Only in the case of *Alcazar* do we have both printed play and plot, and these together manage to indicate both the acts and scenes. The plot indicates indirectly both acts and scenes. The printed play indicates indirectly the acts, and, in addition,

23 For the payments, see *Henslowe's Diary,* ed. W. W. Greg II, 202; for the custom, see below, pp. 29 ff.

numbers and names directly two of the acts. Evidently Peele wrote *Alcazar* in acts. Since these plots were forced to recognize the act-divisions because of music, presenter, or dumb-show (Pope's music and masques, but no monsters, borrowed no doubt from Jonson) which had to be fitted into the sequence of the action, there is no indication whatever that the plays which lacked these features were not written in acts. But it is also true in these other cases that the actors had no need either to mark the act-divisions in any other manuscripts which may have been made specifically for stage purposes. There were simply no externalities to be inserted in the act-intervals for these plots, hence no reason to indicate them in other manuscripts purely for the stage. And there was no other reason to distinguish the intervals between medial scenes from those on either side of an act-division. Scenes were basic stage units, whatever their position. Only literary custom determined that scenes should be subdivided into five groups called acts, and it was "mere convention" only which determined whether these five groups should be marked on the stage by four hiatuses, of whatever length and however marked.

In the case of *Alcazar*, it is all but certain that there was at least one intermediate undivided manuscript between Peele's original, which was certainly divided into acts, and the theatrical plot, which has no specific trace of division into acts as such. Because of the very nature and necessities of making these plots Sir Walter Greg concludes "that in general act division was not formally recorded either in the prompt books or in the Plots of the companies from which specimens of the latter have reached us."[24] That is, the plot of *Alcazar* was itself pretty certainly made, not from Peele's divided original, but from some undivided copy prepared for stage purposes. It will be remembered that surviving nonautograph "Prompt-Books" are

24 Greg, *Dramatic Documents*, p. 80.   26 W. W. Greg, *Henslowe Papers*, p. 67.
25 Greg, *First Folio*, pp. 144–45.

in effect of the undivided form, even where the act-divisions are preserved in the left margin; and we shall soon see that nearly all surviving "Prompt-Books" of this early period were undivided. Such undivided stage-copy would explain why the majority of early quartos were undivided; they would be, not from the author's divided original, but from undivided stage copies deriving from that original. Conversely, lack of division in theatrical plots and stage copies gives no indication whatever that the author did not write his plays in acts and scenes, numbered. Five, if not all seven, of our theatrical plots bear witness to that.

The plots owe their survival to Edward Alleyn of the Admiral's complex of companies, and Sir Walter Greg records, "Act-division was evidently recognized in the Lord Admiral's company before the end of the sixteenth century, for on 23 October 1598 Henslowe paid money 'vnto m^r Chapmane on his playe booke & ij ects of a tragedie of bengemens plotte'."[25] This entry takes on further significance when put into the background of the custom of payments at the period, which is clearly stated some years later in Henslowe's agreement in 1613 with Daborne for *Michael and the Devil*.[26] Daborne was to receive "xx^{ty} pounds, six pounds whearof ye sd Robert aknowledgeth to hav receaved in earnest of ye sayd play . . . & must hav other four pound vpon delivery in of 3 acts, & other ten pound vpon deliuery in of ye last scean *p*fited." This was the normal procedure, though, of course, collaboration and the impecunious importunity of playwrights frequently caused deviations from the rule. Further, in 1598 the total sum for a play was normally around £8, and the proportional amounts accordingly.

So to proceed with Chapman, on January 4, 1598, he received £3 "vpon iij ackes of a tragedie,"[27] followed January 8 by £3 in full payment. In view of the custom, it is clear that on

27 *Henslowe's Diary*, ed. W. W. Greg, I, 100.

October 23, 1598, Chapman received £3 for having done some writing on two acts, as piecework, on Jonson's plot[28] and in earnest of a tragedy he himself was to write, the proportion being doubtless the regular £2 in earnest and £1 for his patch-work. He then received £3 payment on the first three acts January 4, 1599, followed by full payment of £3 January 8. It is easy to demonstrate for plays and playwrights generally that this was the custom of the company by 1598, when a shift in business arrangements had caused Henslowe to begin keeping accounts of these payments. The custom was fully established, and must have been in existence long before. Certainly long before 1598 the plays for the Admiral's men had been written and paid for in acts.[29] We may add that the manuscript of Mundy's *Kent*, 1590, which belongs also somewhere in the Admiral's complex, is divided into acts. Surely it is clear from all this evidence that authors for the Admiral's complex in the nineties distinguished and numbered at least their acts, just as authors did in every known surviving autograph thereafter, or, for that matter, as ordinary copyists also did with almost equal unanimity. It was the literary thing to do.

And, by the same token, the custom of writing in acts was not confined to the Admiral's. It is at least amusing to find that just as Chapman had completed in 1598 a play on "bengemens plotte," so Jonson himself the previous year had completed a play begun by Nashe. This play, the *Isle of Dogs,* completed for Pembroke's men at the Swan in July, 1597, was also cer-tainly put together in acts. Nashe calls it an "imperfit Embrion of my idle houres. . . . An imperfit Embriō I may well call it, for I hauing begun but the induction and first act of it, the other foure acts without my consent, or the least guesse of my drift

28 Since the acts were two, one would suspect that they were the last two, to finish a play which "bengemen" had engineered past the first three acts be- fore he had to take time out to read his neck-verse. The show must go on.

29 For a brief sketch of the play process, see Baldwin, *Organization and Per-*

or scope, by the players were supplied, which bred both their trouble and mine to."[30]

Nashe would first have had the approval of the players on his plot before he began to write. Presumably this plot also was written, and it would be but the barest sketch of the proposed matter of the play. On this plan, he had written and evidently handed in the induction and the first act. For some reason, not stated or so far inferable, the players without Nashe's consent—whether against his will is not stated—then had Jonson supply the final four acts—and both the players and Jonson landed in prison for their pains, where Nashe had no mind to join them. Since at most the players would have had but a sketchy plot from Nashe, he is within reason in saying that they had proceeded without "the least guesse of my drift or scope"—they had no way of knowing how Nashe would have developed his plot—his "drift or scope." If the offensive matter was in those last four acts, Nashe certainly could not be held responsible—as apparently he was not. Certainly, here was a play actually constructed for Pembroke's in five acts.

Jasper Mayne gives some hint at the probable difficulties here of the players, when he takes a turn on Jonson's "blots."

> *Scorne then their censures who gav't out,* thy Witt
> *As long upon a* Comœdie *did sit*
> *As* Elephants *bring forth; and that* thy blotts
> *And* mendings *tooke more time then* Fortune *plotts.*[31]

Here "Fortune *plotts*" is an evident reference to the whole process of working out the plot to the completed play, where Jonson took more time for "blotts *And* mendings" (such as he thought Shakspere would have been the better for having made) than writers for the Fortune took for writing a whole

sonnel, pp. 300–303, also ed. *Comedy of Errors* (1928), pp. vi–vii.
30 R. B. McKerrow, *Nashe,* III, 153–54; E. K. Chambers, *Elizabethan Stage* I, 298; II, 132, 151.
31 *Jonsonus Virbius,* 1638, p. 30; Herford & Simpson, I, 186.

play. Since the company had passed the play, this slow final process would be particularly annoying, especially since the polishing would mean little to the version they would actually perform. According to Jonson, as well as Heminges and Cundall, Shakspere did not by "blotts *And* mendings" cause delay.

Now that the plots have shown us certain fundamentals of stage practice at their date, it will be well to examine narrowly the practice in the surviving nonautograph "Prompt-Books" from Shakspere's active days, since these are copies, made presumably for stage purposes. Of the nonautograph early plays, *Richard II* or *Thomas of Woodstock*, (*c.* 1592–95), "As originally written . . . was undivided except for '(1) Sceane' at the beginning and '2 sceane' on fol. 162ᵇ. But another hand has introduced a full division into acts by adding the necessary notes in the margin."[32] The original from which this copy was made evidently had the acts and scenes numbered, and these indications were supposed to be omitted in copying; but the first two scene-indications slipped through, and the act-notations were added by another hand in the margin, the only attributions to this hand.[33] The process by which this copy of *Woodstock* was made is thus an exact analogue of that employed in Massinger's *Believe As Ye List,* where the act and scene headings were cut, but act-notations added in the left margin. Only, in *Woodstock* these act and scene headings were in the original, but cut in copying, and then the act-notations were put in the margin of the copy. As to the date of the copy of *Woodstock*, "The writing might be as early as *c.* 1590, it might be a full generation later."[34] As we have seen, Sir Walter prefers *c.* 1592–95 for the play. At what time "another hand," not otherwise known in the play, introduced the "full division into acts" is not ap-

32 Greg, *Dramatic Documents,* p. 253.   34 Frijlinck, *M. S. R.,* p. vii.
33 Wilhelmina P. Frijlinck, ed., *Malone*   35 Greg, *Dramatic Documents,* p. 253.
   Society Reprint, pp. xii, xv.

parent from Sir Walter's description, for "into the complex question of the differentiation of the various revisional hands, and of their chronological relation . . . it is impossible to enter here."[35] But Sir Walter connects some of these alterations with *Charlemagne, The Second Maiden's Tragedy,* and *Sir John Barnavelt,* where he suspects Sir George Buck. The marginal notations for acts may, therefore, have been inserted many years later than the putative date of the play, *c.* 1592–95, which may or may not be the date of the surviving copy of the manuscript.

In our next nonautograph, these marginal notations are said definitely to have been inserted later. *Edmond Ironside* (1590–1600?) "As originally written . . . was wholly undivided, but a later hand has effected a division into acts by adding the required notes in the left margin. It is noticeable that the direction 'Act 4' is placed at the foot of the page after Act III, not at the head of Act IV."[36] It is not stated directly in the description whether the "later hand" which "effected the division into acts" was one of those concerned "in a late revival . . . most likely . . . somewhere in the twenties,"[37] but since only one stage reviser is involved and these annotations are said to be in his hand,[38] it would appear to be clear that they were added "somewhere in the twenties." If so, then these stage divisions were pretty certainly inserted later than the date of the copy, though that copy "might have been written at any time within a generation or so before or after 1600."[39] At least, here is a copy made without division in the text and kept so for stage purposes, but with act-divisions indicated in the margin later, either relative to the time of copying the text, or at some later reworking.

The Second Maiden's Tragedy, licensed October 31, 1611,

36 Greg, *Dramatic Documents,* p. 258.   38 E. Boswell, *M.S.R.,* p. vii.
37 Greg, *Dramatic Documents,* p. 257.   39 Boswell, *M.S.R.,* p. vi.

has "division into acts only, which are marked in the left margin. Though the scenes are not numbered or recognized in any formal manner, they are indicated through most of the play by the position of the directions."[40] That is, the exemplar from which this copy was made indicated the scenes, and doubtless the acts, in the text. But in the copy the act-notations have been made in the margin, and the scenes have not been formally indicated as such.

Another manuscript belongs in Class A, which we are considering, if that class is to be "Prompt-Books," though this manuscript has been placed under Class C, "Some other Manuscripts of Interest." This is the particularly interesting *John of Bordeaux* (1590–1600?). "Marginal directions by a playhouse reviser, which thrice include the name of John Holland, make it clear that the manuscript has served as a prompt book; but in most respects it differs widely from the normal type."[41] It is, however, normal as to one stage type, as established above, in that it is wholly undivided. Since this manuscript would have been a most excellent "bad" quarto, had it been printed, as now it has been, it is of peculiar interest to know of this variant type. Further, *John of Bordeaux* survives untampered and completely undivided, being also probably the earliest of our instances, since John Holland, whose name occurs three times in it, is found in other plays of the early nineties, including the undivided *2 Henry VI,* as printed in the First Folio. For in the case of the undivided *2* and *3 Henry VI,* "We can point to a few actors' names that seem to owe their presence to the book-keeper."[42] Evidently, *2* and *3 Henry VI* were

40 Greg, *Dramatic Documents*, pp. 265–66.

41 Greg, *Dramatic Documents*, p. 355.

42 Greg, *First Folio*, p. 119.

43 There are no early undivided plays in Class B; and *Tancred and Ghismonda, c.* 1600? of Class C, "seems to be purely literary" (Greg, *Dramatic Documents*, p. 356).

44 Sir Walter Greg himself now makes this grouping. "Most playhouse manuscripts show some sort of division. Of nineteen that we need take account of, only *More* and *John of Bordeaux* are wholly undivided, but in the case of *Woodstock* (in which originally only the first and second scenes were

printed, directly or by copy, from the original undivided copy made for the stage in the early 'nineties, presumably because no more authentic, divided copies were available. Incidentally, if we knew what happened to *John of Bordeaux,* that would go far toward explaining what happened to the manuscripts underlying the "bad" quartos of *2* and *3 Henry VI.*[43]

These four instances now make it clear that the anomalous and by this time notorious *More,* in Mundy's autograph, also belongs with them, since it is a wholly undivided "Prompt-Book," and no one has troubled at any time to add the act-notations in the margin.[44] So also does the autograph *Charlemagne* (*c.* 1605?) belong. "The division is into acts only, though in each case the heading mentions the first scene as well. That to Act I is centred; the others are in the left margin."[45] Apparently the indications in the left margin are in the same hand as the text. But the "stage reviser" has inserted "Actus 2" in the left margin, in fact deleting "Act⁹ 2 Sce: 1," whether intentionally or not. The jotting was probably the result of an automatic reflex only.

Thus the two definitely early manuscripts, *More* and *Bordeaux,* have no trace of division. The two definitely later, *Charlemagne* and *Second Maiden's Tragedy,* insert the markings in the left margin at copying, the copy in each case being evidently from a fully divided manuscript. In the other two cases, it seems probable for *Ironside* that the stage revisions of the twenties, including act-divisions, were inserted upon an undivided manuscript copy of several years earlier. The same may be true of *Woodstock.* In fact, then, all surviving "Prompt-

marked) and of *Ironside* the present division into acts is a later importation. All four are early. The only other sixteenth-century manuscript, *John a Kent,* has an original division into acts only" (Greg, *First Folio,* p. 143). While playhouse manuscripts generally show some sort of division, though not usually in the text, yet most early ones, before 1600, do not; and these are for our purposes the important ones. For the quartos, at least, it might be well to forget entirely for a while the later manuscripts, with their undivided divisions.

45 Greg, *Dramatic Documents,* p. 262.

Books" through 1611 are undivided as to text, except Mundy's autograph *Kent;* that is, six out seven. The custom of inserting the act-numbering in the margin for stage purposes would thus appear to have originated at some time in the seventeenth century. Earlier copies made for stage purposes omitted division entirely, as plots did. But plots would indicate in various ways when inserts were to be made at act-divisions. Presumably the manuscripts would do the same, and presumably they did when occasion arose. In surviving instances, there was no reason to preserve these divisions, and they were not preserved. But for some reason, which need not trouble us here, in the seventeenth century it became advisable to know where these act-divisions were, and so the text of the copies still remained undivided but these act-notations were inserted in the margin. Even a fully divided autograph, as was Massinger's *Believe As Ye List,* might have the original divisions within the text obliterated, and the act-notations put in the margin.

One noticeable fact about this group of early manuscripts is that while the copies are for the stage, they are neither autograph nor the original licensed copies. In *John of Bordeaux,* there is no trace of censor or of license. Nor is there any in *Ironside.* In *Woodstock,* "certain alterations have been made in deference to the censor, if not by the censor himself."[46] But if so, there is no license (though the apparent loss of a last page might account for this), and these alterations were made later than the original manuscript. While Sir Walter Greg finds that in *Charlemagne* "One passage has certainly been censored . . . seems to be in the hand of Sir George Buc,"[47] yet there is no license. Only with *The Second Maiden's Tragedy,* do we reach what is later the normal type of licensed manuscript, though it is not autograph. Of our early group, the undivided autograph *More* alone is being ripped to pieces in the face of a prohibition by Tilney. While, as a group, these are undivided copies of

---

46 Greg, *Dramatic Documents,* p. 252.

manuscripts for stage purposes, they are not initially the censored and licensed copies, and even if eventually censored by
or in accordance with the directions of the Master of the Revels,
were yet never the licensed copies. As a matter of fact, we
have no instance of a licensed copy till *The Second Maiden's
Tragedy* in 1611, and can not prove directly, so far as I
know, that it had been the custom earlier to attach the license
to the manuscript. It would, at any rate, seem clear that besides the licensed manuscript, if there were one, be it autograph
or itself a copy, companies required for acting purposes at least
an undivided copy, and that this undivided copy, as we shall see,
is the form which underlies the majority of early printed quartos.

Another fact to be borne in mind is that these early stage
manuscripts of all kinds are but lightly edited by "stage-
revisers." Though *John of Bordeaux* was not granted a place
among "Prompt-Books," yet it shows the same kind and
quantity of stage-revision as other early manuscripts. To take
the early autographs among recognized "Prompt-Books," in
More there appears to be no evidence of "the editor's" efforts
upon the original before the cutting was done. In *John a Kent,*
the "stage-reviser" is accused of only four "Enters" and three
"Musiques," all in the left margin for attention. In the autograph *Charlemagne, c.* 1605, Sir Walter puts stars on fourteen
jottings, and in the nonautograph but licensed *Second Maiden's
Tragedy* of 1611 thirteen. In both cases, the nature of the
entries is similar to that of those in *Kent,* except that two actors
are named in *The Second Maiden's Tragedy,* and there is a
little more of necessary stage-business to be attended to in
both *Charlemagne* and *Second Maiden's Tragedy* than in *Kent.*
In Sir Walter's notes, we do not begin to "see stars" in any
profusion for the "stage-reviser's" additions till *Barnavelt,*
1619.

Such sparse annotations could be, and in the seventeenth

47 Greg, *Dramatic Documents,* p. 261.

century sometimes were, indicated upon print.[48] Malone described one such copy with sufficient accuracy for our purposes, being a 1599 quarto of *Romeo and Juliet,* at that time belonging to Steevens, now at Yale. "It has been thought by some that our author's dramas were exhibited without any pauses, in an unbroken continuity of scenes. But this appears to be a mistake. In a copy of *Romeo and Juliet,* 1599, now before me, which certainly belonged to the play-house, the endings of the acts are marked in the margin; and directions are given for musick to be played between each act. The marginal directions in this copy appear to be of a very old date, one of them being in the ancient style and hand—'*Play musicke.*' "[49] This quarto was certainly at some time used to record certain stage notes. Apparently Malone thought that these go back to Shakspere's own time, and it seems clear enough that they are at least of the seventeenth century. At any rate, any quarto of the time might well have been so used, whether this one, or any one, actually was in that time so used or not.

So sparse were these annotations of the early "stage-revisers" that they might be attached to the theatrical plots. Four of the seven plots (*Dead Man's Fortune, Troilus and Cressida, Battle of Alcazar, 1 Tamar Cam*) have such annotations of the same types as in the early stage copies, except that the minor actors are cared for within the plot, though in *The Dead Man's Fortune* at one place an omission to mention the names of a group of three is repaired by mention in the margin, while at another the names are squeezed in. In these four cases, the "prompter" was thus prepared to "prompt" without a "copy." That is, such notations did not belong necessarily to the actual process of prompting, but were to be looked after by some other individual or individuals than the actual book-holding prompter, who obviously must have had a copy

48 My colleague, Professor G. B. Evans, will furnish various instances of prompt on print in a forthcoming volume or volumes.

of the play. In this system, then, certainly more than one manuscript was involved, as probably was the case in any actual system of the time. At any rate, we can never without proof assume for any play either that there was only one manuscript or that there was only one type of manuscript.

A literary reference gives the function of these plots. "How were the actors to learn and keep up with their entrances, exits, etc., without bedevilling the life out of the poor prompter? Marston gives us the clue in the second part of *Antonio and Mellida,* IV. 1. 226–27, when Antonio says in stage terms:

> *quick observation, scud*
> *To cote the plot, or else the path is lost.*

There was thus a plot which the actors were themselves to consult in case of doubt."[50] *Antonio and Mellida* was "by the children of Paules," and "observation" may have been a deputy of the prompter, but more likely was one of the actors, this being a self-help device.

In the preceding four instances, there must have been at least "The Booke and Platt" of the play as in *2 The Seven Deadly Sins.* But in this latter plot, as also in *Frederick and Basilea,* and apparently *2 Fortune's Tennis,* there are no such "stage-reviser's" annotations in the margins. For these three plays, these annotations must have been on the accompanying "Booke" in each case. The "booke" used with a plot, therefore, might be without all prompt annotations, as apparently were *Woodstock* and *Ironsides* originally, whether they were used with a plot or not. But since the plot always contained within itself originally, or supplementally within or in the margin, the necessary annotations for minor actors, this feature would not be found in the accompanying manuscript. Conversely, plays with minor actors named, as are several of Shakspere's, were

49 Malone, *Shakespeare* (1790), Vol. I, Part II, p. 93, *n.* 9. 50 Baldwin, *Organization and Personnel,* pp. 143–44.

not used with a plot. For Shakspere, Sir Edmund Chambers lists, "*2, 3 Hen. VI, Tam. of Shrew, Rom. & Jul., Mid. N. Dr., 2 Hen. IV, Hen. V, Much Ado, All's Well*" as having actor's names.[51] Among surviving manuscripts for the nineties, *John of Bordeaux* has annotations for one actor at least, and *More* was acquiring such annotations at revision.

Theoretically, the "booke" could have been the author's autograph or some kind of copy. We have but two autographs of the period of the surviving plots, both by Mundy. The "Booke" of *More* appears to have been originally without "stage-reviser's" annotations, but the "Booke" of *Kent* has sparse notes. Neither of these, of course, is known to have had any actual connection with plots.

The chief reason for this early bareness of addition against later profusion is also clear. To consider Shakspere's company, by the twenties it was a large organization, with functions rather elaborately differentiated and systematized. The struggling organization for which Shakspere wrote the majority of his quarto plays in the nineties was quite a different set-up. The stage officials of that early day simply could not take time to improve the author's manuscript. There is no sign of the elaborate planning and polishing by various officials, which in the later manuscripts is the delight of our paleographic hearts. Under such early conditions, we would also expect the author to permit himself more laxity, and the officials, too, to be more lax—should we say, more rough and ready?—in shaping the author's manuscript for the stage. It may be that the author himself was "fouler" and was foully permitted to stay so. Evidently we need to center attention upon the early manuscripts, plots, quartos, etc. for the men's companies generally in

---

51 E. K. Chambers, *William Shakespeare,* I, 237, *n. 2.*

52 "We can hardly be far wrong in saying that, of plays acted by men's companies in the public theatres [1591–1610], the undivided texts are four times as numerous as the divided" (W. W. Greg, "Act-Divisions in Shakespeare," *RES* (1928), IV, 157). Sir Walter finds no difference in this respect between the Chamberlain's and the Admiral's companies. He

order to form a relevant and relative background for studying the quartos of Shakspere's plays.

Except for Mundy's autograph *Kent,* all "Prompt-Books" before 1605, if *Charlemagne* is that early, appear to have been not only undivided but also without any notations of act-divisions. Consequently, this is the ordinary form of the quartos printed before King James. If one examines the details now so abundantly yet frugally supplied by Sir Walter Greg's unsurpassed and probably never to be equalled bibliography, he will find that academic plays, including those for children's companies, are normally printed in acts and usually in scenes. But of the plays for men before the reign of James, only about one-fourth are divided into acts, and less than a third of those are divided into scenes.[52] Here, as usual, Sir Walter has the clinching information, in his observation upon the "booke called the booke of" for three plays entered S. R., Peele's *David and Bethsaba* (May 14, 1594), Shakspere's *Merchant of Venice* (October 28, 1600), and Shakspere's(?) *Pericles* (May 20, 1608).[53] In the case of *Merchant,* this form has been induced in a significant way. The provisional entry of July 22, 1598 had described it as "a booke of," so that the transfer naturally refers to it as "A booke called the booke of." Numerous plays are called "a booke," though they had no monopoly on the term. Being from "the booke," whether the actual "booke" or a copy of it which preserved the title, these plays are undivided in print. But "the booke" could be at least partly divided. "The Book of Iohn A kent & Iohn a Cumber" in Mundy's autograph is divided into acts; but "The Booke of Sir Thomas Moore," also equally in Mundy's autograph, is not divided at all.

So the author's own manuscript, which would regularly

himself warns, however, that he is on less safe ground when he assumes that the printed plays probably reflect accurately the corresponding prompt-books. W. T. Jewkes, *Act-Division in* *Elizabethan and Jacobean Plays 1583-1616* has now "put all the data together" to approximately the same statistical conclusions.

53 Greg, *Dramatic Documents,* p. 192.

be marked as to acts and frequently as to scenes could be used as "the booke," as in Mundy's *Kent;* but surviving instances indicate that in these early days usually a copy was made, with all divisions supposed to be eliminated from the text, even if the copy is autograph, as Mundy's *More.* The majority of plays printed in this period descend from this undivided type of copied "booke," as do all of the quartos for Shakspere's plays, except the late *Othello, 1622.* Incidentally, *Merchant* and *Pericles* advertize properly on their title pages "as acted." These quartos are from the undivided "booke," as acted, not from Shakspere's autograph, or an unedited copy of it. Quite properly, Heminges and Cundall caused most of the plays in these quartos to be checked for the First Folio to divided manuscripts, which they considered to be, or to be as good as, Shakspere's own unblotted originals. Whether that assumption be true or not, at least in thus preserving the divisions, these manuscripts were closer to those originals.

It is now clear that any professional dramatist of the time wrote in acts and scenes, and that always he numbered his acts, usually his scenes, or at least he indicated them in other ways. But the evidence of the surviving plots and manuscripts, as well as of the early quartos, makes it certain that copies of plays made for the theatrical purposes of the men's companies were frequently undivided, though in the plots act-divisions would be otherwise indicated if there were to be inserts at them, and the same could have been true of the manuscripts, though we have no surviving manuscript of a kind to necessitate this. Thus the uniform practice in surviving plots, manuscripts, and quartos makes it as certain as evidence can that the quartos of Shakspere's plays were printed from undivided stage copies, or copies of them. And two of them are so labeled. *The Merchant of Venice,* and *Pericles* (if Shakspere's,) are branded with "the booke," and regularly the advertisement for these quartos is "as played." That much we now know.

From this examination based upon manuscripts and plots, one thing is clear throughout the period to the closing of the theaters. The actors did not expect to observe act-divisions as such. But it is also equally clear that in more than half the plots the stage officials knew where the act-divisions were when they had any reason to know, and presumably knew or could have known in the other instances had it been useful to know. Similarly, in the surviving manuscripts, with rare exception, this information concerning the position of act-divisions is preserved, but where the stage official has anything to do with it, then inconspicuously and not in the text. Acts as such were never at this period of any fundamental importance to those who prepared plays for the stage. Only if an interval was to occur between acts to accommodate some form of insertion did these officials become actively interested. Such a manuscript as the undivided autograph *More* by Mundy would have been completely satisfactory to them for that play. So would the undivided quartos of early days have been, whether those for Shakspere, or those for other writers, most of which get the same treatment. In early days, they would keep them so; later they would make act-notations in the left margin.

It is now evident that we must distinguish between "merely conventional" literary divisions, compositional and rhetorical in nature, and the observance of such divisions on the stage, which was also "merely conventional." While, for acting, the scene-divisions are the smallest common denominator, they are not preserved, even in theatrical plots, to show either continuity between scenes or the lack of it, but merely the sequence of scenes, together with the sequence of actors and action in each, in that way also indicating indirectly the whole sequence of action. Scenes are not necessarily dividers any more than acts are. The action can be absolutely continuous, in time at least, throughout, whether the compositional units are marked or not. The compositional units need not be in any way distinguished for the stage or on the stage. Staging could wholly ignore these units; it could observe any or all of them by any method it knows or can devise.

Also, because the scenes in Shakspere's time were normally constructed as separate units and did not differ in construction whether medial or at the end of the rhetorical act, their order could sometimes be rearranged. And if one chose, he could make a stage pause of whatever length coincide with the ending of any scene, not merely with the ending of a scene which happened to be at the end of the rhetorical act.[54] As we have seen above, even the scene-division upon which the act-division fell might be but hazily indicated.

54 Prompt on print will show various instances of variant act-division markings in the seventeenth century. See, for instance, the Steevens copy of the 1599 *Romeo and Juliet,* now at Yale, and others described in forthcoming work of my colleague, Professor G. B. Evans.

Chapter Three

COMEDIES WITH ACTS AND SCENES

MARKED IN THE FIRST FOLIO

WE NOW HAVE some indication of how to interpret act and scene headings as they appear in the First Folio. Since these ideas of form were developed under the impulsion of Latin comedy, specifically Terence, it is natural that in the First Folio Shakspere's comedies come nearest to conforming to "correctness" of form as understood in his day. We shall, therefore, confine our basic discussion to them. All fourteen comedies attempt to discriminate the acts, though Capell was not pleased with the irregularity of *Shrew;* no more is Dover Wilson. Seven of the fourteen comedies (*Tempest, Gentlemen, Wives, Measure, Like It, Night, Tale*) divide not only into acts but also into scenes. These are seven of the ten comedies first printed in the First Folio from manuscript, and belong to our first class.

A further characteristic shows that at least three of these seven (*Gentlemen, Wives, Tale*) were copies, to some extent edited by some official or employee. These three comedies normally mass the characters at the scene-headings in addition to numbering acts and scenes. Professor F. P. Wilson has pointed out[1] that a manuscript of Middleton's *Game at Chess* (Malone 25, Bodleian) in the handwriting of Ralph Crane has such mass groupings. This manuscript is also a shortened version,

1 F. P. Wilson, "Ralph Crane," 4 *Library,* VII, 194ff.

omitting by Wilson's count some 760 lines. It would appear
to be evident, however, that Crane is not necessarily responsible
for these divergencies, since another copy made by him of the
same play (Lansdowne 690, B.M.) is of the full form and in
acts and scenes, as a nonacting copy from author's manuscript
should be. Wilson's careful analysis of several other copies of
plays in Crane's handwriting shows that Crane was simply a
very competent professional scrivener, who found some em-
ployment in copying plays, the surviving copies in his hand
being intended usually for patrons, only occasionally for the
actors themselves, though Crane implies that he had done considerable work for them, and the bibliographers have been
busily tracking him in the snow of the First Folio.

Professor Bald has brought another important instance to
light in Webster's *Duchess of Malfy* as printed in 1623. "*The
Dutchesse of Malfy* has the same massed stage directions at
the head of each scene, although the names of the characters
who come on to the stage are not preceded by the word *Enter*
—an omission probably made (perhaps by Webster himself)
in order to approximate more closely to Ben Jonson's neo-classi-
cal practice. There are very few stage directions within the
scenes, but most of these are rather striking in character, and
seem to be explanatory notes added by Webster. The dedication, and the declaration on the title-page that this is 'The perfect and exact Coppy, with diverse things Printed, that the
length of the Play would not beare in the Presentment,' make
it clear that the play was, to some extent at least, seen through
the press by the author [since he was active in its publication],
and he, rather than any one else, is most likely to have been

2 R. C. Bald, " 'Assembled' Texts," 4
   Library, XII, 244–45.
3 Cf. Greg's note, *Ibid.,* p. 248, "An instance of the massing of entrances occurs in the first scene of *Believe as
   you List,* preserved in Massinger's

autograph manuscript (1631)." Such
isolated instances might, however, be
the result of accident. There is also
an isolated instance in *1 Henry IV,*
I, 2 of the First Folio, changed from
Q. This play is exceptional also

responsible" for various notes.[2] One should take notice positively that though the title-page of Webster's *Duchess of
Malfy,* with Webster at least looking on, claims to print "The
perfect and exact Coppy," yet it has had its scene headings
thrown into the "classical" form, shows characteristic quirks
of punctuation which are alleged to be by Crane as copyist, etc.
Evidently, "perfect and exact" are not used with the same accuracy of denotation that a modern bibliographer would wish.
Since it will appear that Heminges and Cundall are in this same
specific tradition, it will be well not to overlook this established
fact when anyone attempts to interpret their words.[3]

Without saying yea or nay to some of the details, we have
here for the King's men another play divided into acts and
scenes, with massed scene-headings, and this play claims to be
the complete copy, not the cut version. But Ben Jonson's neoclassical practice is not responsible for these characteristics of
the group any more than Crane is. For the characteristic of
massed headings was not even an invention of English drama.
This was the regular method used in the editions of Terence
and Plautus, deriving from manuscript practice.[4] In *Gentlemen*
and *Wives,* the principle is perhaps as well observed as it can be
in a play written under a different system. For normally in English drama of the period, and nearly, if not always, in Shakspere, the scene ends only with a clear stage, while in strict neoclassical theory it should have changed every time the grouping
of the characters changed, though some would permit medial
exits. Even in *Gentlemen,* therefore, we find an occasional exit
medially (permitted by some) and in *Wives* an entrance (never
permissible), all presumably as a grudging concession to this

among the histories in that while it is
divided into acts and scenes, yet its
text conforms to its "good" quarto, the
only history play to do so. As a matter
of fact, it is the only play of the first
class to do so. These aberrations may

mean that it was, at least initially,
prepared for print by those who prepared the comedies.

4 Baldwin, *Five-Act Structure,* p. 99, n.
See quotation above, p. 4 ff.

feature of English practice. Else they are overlooked vestigial survivals. There are a few such medial touches in the Malone copy of *Chess*. But in *Tale* we get two systems. While headings are massed throughout the play, yet for much of it the usual notations also appear. In the light of the origins of the system, it seems clear that someone has imperfectly adapted the old form of *Tale* to the "classical" system, as seems probably the case in *The Duchess of Malfy* also. For in *Tale* there is no harmonization of the two systems, as there is, for instance, in Jonson's practice, which adapts this classical system.[5] In *Chess* the system is found in a cut version, and Professor J. Dover Wilson has insisted with circumstance in his edition of *Two Gentlemen* that there has been considerable cutting from the text of that play as it was printed in the First Folio. But Sir Walter Greg has surely shown in his edition of the "poor" quarto that the folio *Merry Wives* has not been so cut, as does also the length of the latter version. Similarly *Tale* can hardly be a cut version. And *Malfy* claims on the best possible authority to be the full uncut version. The characteristic of massed scene-headings is not peculiar to cut versions.

The appearance of this characteristic in a few plays of the First Folio, 1621–23, in *Malfy*, 1623, and in a copy of *Chess*, 1624, would indicate that some person attached to the King's men 1621–24, whose business it was to edit copy for some purpose, preferred this "classical" characteristic. In *Chess*, his work appears in a cut form, whether he himself had done the cutting from the full form, and whether that full form already contained the editing before it was cut. The sequence would indicate that for this characteristic the editing of *Gentlemen* and *Wives* was done thoroughly and at leisure, whether or not the editor also made the copies. If Crane was the copyist, as sus-

---

5 Greg lists two manuscripts, *Timon* (*Dramatic Documents,* pp. 308–11), *c.* 1600 (?) and *The Queen of Cor-* *sica,* by F. Jaques, 1642 (*Ibid.,* pp. 352–55) as having the "foreign method"; but neither has anything to

pected, of any of these plays, then as in *Chess* he was presumably not the "classical" editor.

While, therefore, these three comedies (*Gentlemen, Wives, Tale*) have act and scene divisions indicated, they appear certainly to be copies already edited as to massed scene headings. These three are tied together by still another editorial aberration; the "lavish use of parentheses and hyphens,"[6] a habit also to be found in *Tempest* and *Measure*. Because this characteristic appears in some of the manuscript copies by Crane, it also, like the massed scene headings, has been attributed to him. But whether the "lavish use of parentheses and hyphens" belongs to Crane, to the "classical" editor, or to someone else, it ties these five plays together as copies to some degree edited. Thus five of these seven comedies with act and scene divisions marked, and first printed in the First Folio from manuscript were printed from copies, to some degree edited, certainly not directly from Shakspere's manuscript.

As we continue with our seven comedies with acts and scenes marked, at least one other was also a copy. For, three of the seven, *Gentlemen, Measure,* and *Night,* have McKerrow's notably regularized speech-headings, indicating that they too are copies. Two of these, *Gentlemen,* and *Measure* are Crane copies, being thus doubly incriminated, also evidently Crane's copies of copies. So of the seven comedies with act and scene divisions marked, only *Like It* has not so far been shown to be a copy. Not only so, but the massed scene-headings show that *Gentlemen, Wives,* and *Tale* were copies of copies, and McKerrow's regularized speech-headings confirm *Gentlemen,* and add *Measure* as a copy of a copy. So at least four of the five Crane copies are from copies, *Tempest* being Crane's only possible exception.

indicate "that it has been used in the playhouse."

6 Greg, *First Folio,* pp. 217, 335, 356, 415, 418, 426–27.

When the typographers began setting about February 1, 1622, they were given first four plays copied by Ralph Crane, *Tempest, Gentlemen, Wives, Measure,* all with characteristic act and scene divisions marked. The other three comedies with act and scene divisions marked, *Like It, Night,* and *Tale,* were not submitted till the final rounding off of the comedies. Here Hinman's findings on the printing come into play. For, following *Well* the printers turned to the histories, and began with *King John.* "Thus *All's Well that Ends Well,* the twelfth of the fourteen plays in the initial section of the volume, was not at once succeeded by either of the two still unprinted Comedies but by *King John; King John* was followed by *Twelfth Night;* and then came something over half of *Richard II.* Work on *Richard II* was presently given over, however, and the last of the Comedies, *The Winter's Tale,* was printed.[7] "From these facts we can only conclude that for some reason the copy for *Twelfth Night* was not readily available when quire X was finished [though it evidently became so soon afterward], and that the copy for *The Winter's Tale* was in like manner unavailable when quire Z was finished (though on this occasion the want was made good even more quickly than before). The two plays in question had not hitherto been printed; no difficulty over copyright can be supposed—only some short-lived trouble over the copy itself."[8] It was evidently known, however, when quire X was completed that another comedy was to follow, since *Well* had still enough lines left to occupy Y1, recto and verso, and later events make it clear that *Tale* was not the expected play. For even when they completed *Night* the printers made no provision for another comedy, but closed their work with one whole page (Z6ᵛ) blank. It is thus clear that *Night* is the play for which the printers had provided following *Well,* waiting till

7 Hinman, *Printing,* I, 351.
8 Hinman, *Printing,* I, 521.

9 Chambers, *William Shakespeare,* II, 346.

it could be copied. And *Tale* was to them a complete after-thought, even though it had apparently long been copied and came to them so soon after they had completed work on *Night*. It would seem that for some reason *Night* had been out of hand originally, and was now being attached in a copy, though not made by Crane. The delay in printing noted by Hinman was probably caused by the necessity of making this copy, with Crane not available as copyist. Evidently *Night* and *Tale* were attached at the end of the comedies by way of completing their number. Incidentally, this is a guarantee that had Heminges and Cundall been aware of other plays which they considered to be Shakspere's they would have had them also attached.

Tale has sufficient history to indicate the reasons for its laggardness. It had been performed at Court as late as April 7, 1618.[9] There must, therefore, still at that time have been a properly authorized manuscript. But when the company began in August, 1623, to plan a revival, the allowed manuscript was "missinge." Herbert records, "For the king's players. An olde playe called Winter's Tale, formerly allowed of by Sir George Bucke, and likewyse by mee on Mr. Hemmings his worde that there was nothing profane added or reformed, thogh the al-lowed booke was missinge; and therefore I returned it without a fee, this 19 of August, 1623,"[10] The Company was preparing to revive the play, which was selected for court performance. For Herbert also records, "To the Duchess of Richmond, in the kings absence, was given The Winter's Tale, by the K. com-pany, the 18 Janu. 1623. Att Whitehall."[11] If we have any faith left in anyone's accuracy or veracity at that time, it is important to notice that the word of Heminges implies that a faithful copy of the original had been available by August 19, 1623, and had been submitted, even though the "allowed booke"

10 E. Malone, *Variorum* (1821), III, 229. 11 Malone, *Variorum* III, 228.

of the play was missing. Nor is there anything to indicate that this faithful copy of the play had just been discovered. Nor that it was a copy of the "allowed booke."

We do not know at what time between Appril 7, 1618 and August 19, 1623 the "allowed booke" of *Tale* was discovered to be "missinge." It has been supposed by some that printing of the play in the First Folio was the cause or at least the occasion of its disappearance. The manuscript for *Tale* submitted to the printers (late in 1622?) was at least a double copy, with "classical" scene-headings and Crane's characteristics as copyist. It was not, therefore, itself the "allowed booke," which was missing by August, 1623. Instead, it had both act and scene divisions marked, which would indicate that it was in direct descent from the author's autograph.

We now face the question of why Crane did not include a copy of *Tale* with his batch of four copies to start the printers on work. There is nothing to indicate that the "classical" copy used, or some other, was ever unavailable. But there had been a question of classification, which had certainly caused some difficulty. The general scheme of classification for the First Folio was the old conventional triple division of poetry generally, into comedy, history, and tragedy.[12] *Tale* and *Cymbeline* posed a difficult problem for that scheme, then as now; but we dodge the issue by making a fourth classification of tragicomedy.[13] It seems certain, therefore, that *Tale* and *Cymbeline* were necessarily reserved for a final decision as to classification, at whatever stage in the printing process that decision was made. Since *Tale,* "similar to pastoral tragicomedy," even in spite of a few well-glossed deaths early in the play, was from the story books, and ended story-book style in marriage and happily reunited families, it was eventually attached to the

12 See M. T. Herrick, *Tragicomedy,* pp. 215 ff.

13 See M. T. Herrick, *Tragicomedy,* pp. 249, 255–60 for an analysis of the two plays as "tragicomedy," and a statement of the evident fact that "the men who made up the first folio recog-

comedies, while *Cymbeline,* "very like tragedy with a happy ending," being serious "gospel history" like *Lear,* was added at the end of the tragedies. The fact that *Tale* was placed at the end of the comedies and *Cymbeline* at the end of the tragedies shows certainly that those responsible recognized not only a difference between the two plays but also between each play and the type to which it was attached. This decision was evidently the final one on major arrangement, affecting as it did the ending of two of the three major classifications.

Thus the evidence indicates that for *Tale* a copy was at some time made by the "classical" editor, and a copy of his results made by Crane used for the First Folio. Fortunately, the zeal of the "classical" editor had not quite made so perfect a job as in *Gentlemen* and *Wives,* and so the preceding manuscript shows through heavily. The condition of his work here in contrast to that in those two plays would seem to indicate that he was obliged to do a hurry-up job of editing.

One would naturally suspect that the "book-keeper" would in some way be connected with such changes as the "classical" editor has made. It would not be wise, however, to assume that the "book-keeper" in this aspect was only one person. For even if one person was responsible as "book-keeper" for the various functions of the office, it will not do to assume that he performed all these functions in person, especially in so large an aggregation as the King's men. Edward Knight was apparently book-keeper shortly after the events we are studying.[14] Edward Knight "was still with the Prince Charles men in 1623 . . . but appears with the Shakespearean company Dec. 27, 1624."[15] Knight's first surviving work for the King's men appears to have been upon *Honest Man's Fortune,* which was an old play. Herbert noted on the manuscript, "This Play, being an olde One

nized a difference between these two late plays of Shakespeare."
14 J. Gerritsen, *Honest Man's Fortune,* xxi–xxii.
15 Baldwin, *Organization and Personnel,* p. 88.

and thir Originall Lost was reallowd by mee, this: 8. febru.
1624 Att the Intreaty of M^r <Taylor>."[16] The entry in Herbert's office-book is quoted by Malone as "For the king's company. An olde play called The Honest Mans Fortune, the originall being lost, was re-allowed by mee at Mr. Taylor's intreaty,
and on condition to give mee a booke [The Arcadia], this 8
Februa. 1624."[17] The original licensed copy had been lost, and
Knight himself, not the professional copyist Crane, had made this
copy from some other surviving manuscript or manuscripts. If
the surviving manuscript was divided into acts and scenes, Knight
kept only the acts. But Gerritsen believes that between the time
Knight made the present copy and the time when he edited it
for prompting, someone else, so far unidentified, had adapted
it for the stage, which is likely enough.[18] Apparently it was not
Knight's duty in this instance to prepare *Honest Man's Fortune*
for the stage, and there is no certain instance of the "classical"
characteristic after he came to the company. The evidence
causes us to suspect Knight's[19] predecessor as book-keeper in the
company 1621–24, or someone who assisted him. That predecessor and his assistants are of unusual importance to us, since
they were quite likely the chief, if not the only actual editors,
for the First Folio.

Even more important, however, is Thomas Vincent and
his probable ways with the undivided copies which underlie the
quartos. "For the Shakespearean company, John Taylor tells
us 'I my selfe did know one *Thomas Vincent* that was a Book-
keeper or prompter at the Globe play-house neere the Banck-
end in Maid-lane.' Thus Vincent was holding the double office
at some time after the Globe was built in 1599. . . . Our only
other record of Vincent is as a musician in *The Seven Deadly
Sins*, about March 1592, just as Knight appeared in 1624 in
the list of musicians and necessary attendants. It is thus to be

16 Greg, *Dramatic Documents,* p. 288.   18 Gerritsen, *Honest Man's Fortune*
17 Malone, *Variorum* III, 229.   xxvi.

inferred that Vincent was probably already bookkeeper by 1592."[20] Apparently, then, Vincent probably would have prepared most of the copies for the stage which underlie the quartos of Shakspere's plays.

Of the seven comedies with act and scene divisions marked, only *As You Like It* stands apart. It does not have regularized speech-headings as do *Gentlemen, Measure,* and *Night.* It does not have massed scene-headings as do *Gentlemen, Wives,* and *Tale.* It does not name the "actors" as do *Tempest, Gentlemen, Measure,* and *Tale.* Further, it is the only comedy of the first class to get inserted into the comedies of the second class. This peculiarity we shall examine in connection with the plays of the second class.

A further fact now becomes evident. Of the five copies tied together by the characteristics of Crane, *Tale* was not made available till after all the other comedies were in print. The other four of this classification were placed first, the two with massed headings being parenthesized between the two which had only lavish parentheses and hyphens. It would seem a warrantable deduction that copies of these previously unprinted plays had to be specially made for printing, and so were placed first. It would follow that, before printing started, probably around February 1, 1622, available copies of the comedies had been checked far enough to make it clear that special copies would need to be made for at least these four. This checking, and the copying of the four was thus likely done no later than 1621. Those responsible did not simply begin with the first play that came to hand. Why the four should be arranged in their particular order of precedence does not appear from the present type of facts.

Crane copied the four comedies which were placed first. Apparently he made at the same time his only other copy, that

---

19 Greg (*First Folio,* p. 100) does not find Knight traceable in F1.

20 Baldwin, *Organization and Personnel,* p. 124.

of *Tale,* which eventually was attached at the end of the comedies, since his copy was evidently already made when the decision came to attach it, and so caused the printers no considerable delay waiting for it to be made. This would concentrate Crane's work to one period long enough before February 1, 1622, for Crane to copy these five plays. Thus preparation began for publication at latest in 1621.

Copies were, of course, the only sensible solution, if the company wished to keep Shakspere's own manuscripts. Particularly if Shakspere's autograph was in any case the licensed copy, the company would be obliged to keep it or to procure another, if ever again it wished to act the play, witness *Tale.* Most likely, all manuscripts submitted were only expendable copies. At best, the printers were given copies, in some cases if not in all, probably more than one degree removed. Even Crane the faithful is accused, whether justly, yet with circumstance, of unfaithfulness in many things. These men had no idea that it was a crime against posterity to improve Shakspere. In fact, it was their business to improve his work sufficiently to be acted decently upon the stage. Fortunately, only a small, though we think too large, amount of the stage improvement has survived to distress us, since even they recognized that what was wanted was full Shakspere, not the cut stage versions of Shakspere. The chief crow we have to pluck with them is the very black and well-feathered one of the way in which they prepared and put these manuscripts into print.

Chapter Four

THEORIES OF ASSEMBLED TEXTS

THE "classical" characteristic we have just been discussing has led to the modern theories of "assembled texts." Apparently Pope must have the credit of having first suggested that the actors' parts may have been used as copy for publication. "It appears that this edition [F1], as well as the Quarto's, was printed (at least partly) from no better copies than the *Prompter's Book*, or *Piece-meal Parts* [italics Pope's] written out for the use of the actors: For in some places their very names are thro' carelessness set down instead of the *Personae Dramatis:* And in others the notes of direction to the *Property-men* for their *Moveables,* and to the *Players* for their *Entries,* are inserted into the Text, thro' the ignorance of the Transcribers."[1]

This inspired Theobald to make a flourish upon the "Piece-meal Parts." "Many Pieces were taken down in Short-hand, and imperfectly copied by Ear from a *Representation:* Others were printed from piece-meal Parts surreptitiously obtain'd from the Theatres, uncorrect, and without the Poet's Knowledge. . . . When the *Players* took upon them to publish his Works intire, every Theatre was ransack'd to supply the Copy; and *Parts* collected which had gone thro' as many Changes as Performers, either from Mutilations or Additions made to them."[2]

When Dr. Johnson in turn waxed eloquent in 1756 upon

1 Pope, *Shakespear* (1725), I, xvii–xviii.   2 L. Theobald, *Shakespeare* (1733), I, xxxvii–xxxviii.

the imperfections of the quartos only, he inserted Pope into Heminges and Cundall thus: "printed at last without the concurrence of the authour, without the consent of the proprietor, from compilations made by chance or by stealth out of the separate parts written for the theatre: and thus thrust into the world surreptitiously and hastily."[3] Pope had believed that both the Folio and the quartos may have done some compiling from actors' parts. With the words of Heminges and Cundall ringing in his goose-quill, Dr. Johnson applies Pope's theory to the quartos only, to explain the ire of those worthies.

Dr. Johnson did not repeat the doctrine of parts in his Preface in 1765. Capell in 1768 gave Pope's censure short shrift because "his arguments for it are some of them without foundation, and the others not conclusive; and it is to be doubted, that the opinion is only thrown out to countenance an abuse that has been carry'd to much too great lengths by himself and another editor,—that of putting out of the text passages that they did not like."[4]

After quoting Dr. Johnson's *Proposals* of 1756, Malone in 1790 singles out for criticism Dr. Johnson's statement about printing from parts, saying "Nor is it true, in the latitude in which it is stated . . . two only of all his dramas, *The Merry Wives of Windsor* and *King Henry V.* appear to have been thus thrust into the world, and of the former it is yet a doubt whether it is a first sketch or an imperfect copy."[5] These two examples were the "bad" quartos as known at that time. The critics had lost interest in the doctrine of parts, and Malone's limitation upon its possible applicability did not revive discussion.

These various pronouncements passed down the variorum editions without causing any notable ripples. It remained for R. Crompton Rhodes and J. Dover Wilson in modern times to build up simultaneously theories of assembled texts. It will be well to look first at the theory of Rhodes, since it was given separate publication and is thus more clearly formalized. Rhodes has built his theory of "assembled texts" upon the "classical" characteristic. "When an 'allowed book' was missing, by a simple process of scissors and paste they could always assemble the players' parts into one continuous text. In this 'assembled text' the word-cues would be pasted over, and many directions for entrance and exit, while there would be no collective directions. It would consist entirely of dialogue, and therefore be 'less complete,' and though ultimately the insertion of directions might make it indistinguishable from the prompt-book, often there would be traces that the directions have been reconstructed from the context, and they would appear 'less authentic.'

"Clearly, this hypothesis of an assembled text introduces a new factor into Shakespearean bibliography. Fortunately, it is capable of direct illustration. The *Merry Wives of Windsor* in the First Folio has three peculiarities:

i] The entrances of characters are not distributed at the actual places of their appearance on the stage, but collective at the head of each scene.

ii] The only other directions are an 'Exeunt omnes' at the end of each scene.

iii] The text has been set up from obviously legible and intelligible copy. . . .

"The first peculiarity, the list of characters, is easy of explanation: The control of a theatrical performance required two partial transcripts from the prompt-book—(1) a set of parts, complete with cue, dialogue, and certain directions, and (2) a detailed extract from the stage-directions to serve as his remembrancer. Among other things this would contain scene by scene a list of the characters in order of their appearance, so

5 Malone, *Shakespeare* (1790), I, 10.

they could be called to stand by. This was known as the 'platt' or 'plot.'

"Clearly this plot would be a most valuable guide for keeping the players' parts in order, and a transcript of the characters would give a convenient headline to follow. The plot contained no 'business,' that is, action which took place after the entrance had been made on the stage, though it might direct the method of entrance, as 'with lights' or 'with his sword drawn.' No trace of this, however, is found in *The Merry Wives of Windsor*. The omission of 'business' then accounts for the second peculiarity, and also for such calls as for 'musique,' not found in the players' parts.

"The third peculiarity is the natural consequence of printing from the parts, where legibility and intelligibility are essential. Possibly, also, it was due to the Roman script in the players' parts instead of old English, as in the older prompt-books."[6]

Having based his demonstration on *Wives*, Rhodes then illustrates further by *Tale*. "In this play there are some few minor differences which are accounted for by the reconstructor working partly over the directions when pasting his text. While Act IV. Sc. 3 (the Sheep Shearing Feast) is headed, like every other *scena*, by a complete list of characters, those who enter later have their entrances repeated in the proper place, but in general (e.g. Act II. Sc. 1) there are no distributed entrances or exits. Other than the few incidental entrances of minor characters, only five directions have been inserted by the assembler, who, it is plain, recollected a previous performance."[7]

Still further, "The three peculiarities of *The Merry Wives* are reproduced in *The Two Gentlemen of Verona*, while in *Measure for Measure* the entrances are distributed, as they would be in working over a text which had been reconstructed by a more careful use of the plot."[8] "These three assembled

6 R. C. Rhodes, *Shakespeare's First Folio* (1923), pp. 96–98. The gist of this pamphlet had appeared in *T.L.S.*, December 29, 1921, p. 875, as "The

texts [*Gentlemen, Wives, Measure*] appear second, third and fourth in the First Folio, and are uniformly divided into acts and scenes. They form a batch of similar and remarkable texts; there are no other 'assembled' comedies, with the possible exception of *The Comedy of Errors,* the fifth play," another possibility being *A Winter's Tale,* the last of the comedies in the First Folio.[9]

The fact is, of course, that only *Gentlemen, Wives* (neither quite completely), and *Tale* (only partially) show the characteristic stigmata. *Measure* does not, and requires a further hypothesis that, in further working, these have been eliminated. *Errors* is even less cooperative in its actual characteristics. Thus the theory is based primarily on *Wives* and *Gentlemen,* with some support from *Tale.*

Unquestionably, if Rhodes had faced the problem of reconstructing these three comedies, and had available the "plot" and the actors' parts which he demands, he would have done a fair job with scissors and paste of putting together a reasonably complete copy. But Rhodes was not so faced, and there is no known instance in Shakspere's day where anyone did so reconstruct a play, or so far as I know that anyone in that day ever reconstructed one by any method. It is arguable and has been strongly argued that the suggested methods would not have produced present results. But more conclusive, there is no need for such a theory since these three plays are simply edited toward certain current and "proper," "classical" ideas of the time. The stigmata are accounted for by a known contemporary practice. The known takes precedence of the unknown and unnecessary.

Contemporaneous with Rhodes, Professor J. Dover Walson was developing his own theory of assembled texts in the opening volumes (printed 1921) of the principal recent edition

Arrangement of the First Folio."
7 Rhodes, *Folio,* p. 99.

8 Rhodes, *Folio,* p. 100.
9 Rhodes, *Folio,* p. 100–101.

of Shakspere. Here we need only the general statements in the "Textual Introduction" prefixed to *The Tempest,* since the editions of suspected plays simply give for the most part further details of application.[10]

First, we notice some fundamental assumptions as to the role of acts and scenes. "None of the Quartos published during Shakespeare's life-time contains the conventional divisions which now appear in all modern texts. It would seem, therefore, that he did not work in acts and scenes; and the probability that most if not all of these Quartos were printed from prompt-copies suggests that as long as he was at the Globe his plays were performed without breaks. . . . When therefore these divisions occur in Shakespeare's early plays, more especially when, as in *The Taming of the Shrew, King John,* and *1 Henry VI,* they crop up in a very irregular and haphazard fashion, they may be taken as evidence that he was revising other men's work and omitted to delete the act-headings. . . . In short, it seems likely that such act-divisions are theatrical in origin, and arose from the practice of making four pauses during a performance, which were presumably introduced into Shakespeare's prompt-copies after he had left the Globe."[11]

All the assumptions here are contrary to the surviving facts, as we have been examining them above. In the first place, acts and scenes at this period actually and historically belong initially to literary structure, which may or may not be observed on the stage. The numbering of acts and scenes was historically and certainly a matter also of literary form, as were the acts and scenes *per se;* the observance or the nonobservance of pauses between acts and scenes was as certainly a matter of contemporary theatrical practice. And the two things must be

10 In "The Task of Heminge and Condell," *Studies in the First Folio* (1924), pp. 53ff. Professor Wilson recapitulates the theory, with illustrative details. Germinal and seminal leanings are to be found in his series of articles with A. W. Pollard, " 'Stolne and Surreptitious' Shakespearian Texts," *T.L.S.,* January 9, 16, March 13, August 7, 14, 1919. For

sharply differentiated, as they have not been. By Shakspere's time English plays were universally written in acts and scenes, and Shakspere's plays were so written.[12] The plays survive and their structure attests it. Naturally therefore, as we have seen, surviving autographs of other dramatists, even though they have been used for stage purposes, still indicate the acts and scenes, always by numbering the acts, except in Mundy's *More*, and usually by numbering the scenes. Certainly Shakspere constructed in acts and scenes, and there is no reason whatever to suppose that he was the only author of the time who did not mark them. Instead of inserting act and scene divisions, the editors for the stage, at least in surviving manuscripts, usually obliterated these markings in the manuscript, though making their own annotations for the act-division, and in other ways even for scenes. Inevitably, by virtue of the work being done, the dramatist was interested in what happened *within* the acts, the editors for the stage were as inevitably more interested in what happened *between* the acts. Both dramatist and editors were interested in preserving act notations, though the latter found scene headings useless. Irregularities in act and scene divisions do likely indicate some form of interference, and that interference could, of course, originate with the author; but such irregularities would much more likely result from the tinkering of the stage editors, who had a certain prejudice against the literary method of indicating them as mostly useless, and a positive nuisance for their purposes. So in individual cases we must have specific evidence if we are to distinguish between the author and any kind of editor, with his interferences.

The idea that the quartos in their undivided state represent Shakspere's peculiar practice for prompt-copy at the Globe

the suggestion that these massed headings are by "an editor attempting to follow in rather blundering fashion, the scene arrangement of neoclassical plays," see *T.L.S.*, April 19, 1923, p. 254, col. 2.

11 *Tempest*, ed. A. Quiller-Couch & J. D. Wilson, pp. xxxv–xxxvi.

12 See Baldwin, *Five-Act*.

can easily be disposed of. Division or nondivision in print is not a question of the practice of individual authors. Marlowe's *Tamburlaine* (both parts) is divided into acts and scenes. Here Richard Jones, the printer of it, confesses that he is attempting something literary. But all others of Marlowe's plays are undivided, except the academic *Dido*. For Peele, *Arraignment,* for children, is divided into acts and scenes; *Alcazar* is "divided into five acts by the appearance of a Presenter (sometimes with a dumb-show) at the beginning of each, but only the second and fourth marked as such."[13] All others are undivided. For Greene, the putative *Alphonsus* is in acts, as is *James IV,* also with choruses, but *Looking Glasse* (part author) is not in acts, though Oseas serves as chorus to indicate the breaks, and *Bacon* and *Orlando* are undivided. Mundy's two *Huntingdon* plays are undivided, though his autograph *John a Kent* is in acts, but the anomalous *More* is not in either acts or scenes. Jonson's acknowledged plays are, of course, meticulously divided (no compositor was likely to invite Jonson's rapier to get within him). It is not necessary to examine authors further, for it is already clear that for print this is not a question of an individual author who wrote in acts and scenes or of one who did not.

Nor is it a question of the practice of individual companies for men. As we have seen, there is conclusive evidence that the authors for the Admiral's complex in the 'nineties normally wrote in acts. But the plays from this general source

13 W. W. Greg, *Bibliography,* I, 211.
14 Greg, *First Folio,* pp. 144–45; see above, pp. 29 ff.
15 Sir Edmund Chambers says (*Elizabethan Stage,* III, 256), "All make III. iii a Chapman scene, so that, if Chapman spoke the truth, Marston must have interpolated the obnoxious clauses." For Cunliffe, however, this statement is not quite accurate, as Sir Edmund's own summary shows. Cunliffe does give "the first part of Act III to Chapman" (John W. Cunliffe, in C. M. Gayley, *Representative English Comedies,* II, 402), whereas "in the prose I do not detect the mannerisms of Marston until we come to III, iii, containing the passage about the Scots and Virginia, in which . . . they are clearly marked" (II, 403). Herford and Simpson (*Jonson,* IV, 500) continue the near unanimity, "In the third scene of Act III the 'full and heightened style' of Chapman ex-

printed before James show, so far as I can see, at least no higher proportion of division into acts than the general run of so printed plays. Though acts were recognized, as Sir Walter Greg has pointed out[14] in connection with Chapman's work for the Admiral's yet Chapman's two surviving plays for the Admiral's at the same period were undivided in print. These are *The Blind Beggar of Alexandria,* 1596, printed 1598, and *An Humorous Day's Mirth,* 1597, printed 1599. Neither was divided into either acts or scenes. On the other hand, all of Chapman's other plays, which were for children's companies, and so in the erudite tradition, are printed in acts, but not in scenes, numbered, though scenes are indicated by rules in *May Day,* a usual method in manuscripts, perhaps representing Chapman's practice, and though the scenes are numbered in Act III of the collaborated *Eastward Ho.*[15] Chapman, the classicist, would certainly have composed in acts, and his plays for the children's companies were uniformly so printed, but his two plays for the Admiral's were undivided in print, as were, at that time, most of the plays for that company and for all other companies of men.

The authors are not to be blamed for the phenomenon, nor is the practice of the individual companies for men. Nor may we blame individual printers, as a very little unnecessary investigation would show. Nor was it a matter of different theaters for men. Evidently it was a matter of the kind of copy which at that period usually became available to publishers. That kind of

presses itself even in the dishonest rhapsodies of Seagull, and the trick played on Bramble has its counterpart in *All Fools.*" The numbered scene-divisions do not represent Chapman's practice as recorded in print, which was without exception, unless this be it. Marston's plays at this period were usually printed in acts and scenes, as, of course, were Jonson's. The evidence of numbered scenes in only Act III points to Marston or Jonson, and Chapman says Marston was guilty—at least, it was Marston who ran. It is, of course, possible that Marston copied the final fair form of Act III, inserting numbered scene-headings; but that is hardly a plausible procedure. At any rate, this circumstance supports Chapman's statement on the offensive lines against the findings of the majority critics.

manuscript for some three-fourths of all cases for the companies of men before the reign of James had no divisions marked for acts and scenes.[16] Apparently these manuscripts usually did not have even the marginal annotations for acts, as seemingly all surviving early manuscript copies did not, or some printer would occasionally have blundered these into his text.

There is no indication, therefore, that Shakspere "did not work in acts and scenes." Most certainly, he did. Apparently the quartos "were printed from prompt-copies," as suggested, if we define the term suitably; but at this period there seems to be nothing peculiar about the prompt-copies for the Globe to distinguish them from those at other theaters for men. The acquisition of the private Blackfriars may have had some effect upon the form of the prompt-copies, but I know of no conclusive evidence as to what effect. The occurrence or nonoccurrence of divisions in plays can give no direct indication of date and authorship, though it might indirectly have some bearing.

The assumption that Shakspere did not write in acts appears to underlie even one of the super-cautious summaries of Sir Walter Greg. In the case of *Gentlemen,* "More significant, in the circumstances, is the 'Finis' at the end of the first act, which may be compared with the 'Finis, Actus primus' &c. of *Twelfth Night* and suggests that, of the act and scene division, the former at least was not introduced at the time of printing. The division is unlikely to be original, but it is more likely to have been introduced at some later date into the prompt-book than into foul papers. Indeed, foul papers are a very unlikely source in view of the facts that in their own peculiar fashion the directions provide for the presence of all necessary characters (not, however, for re-entries, though exits are sometimes marked) and that there is no irregularity in their designation."[17]

16 See above, pp. 41 ff.   17 Greg, *First Folio,* pp. 217–18.

As I understand it, the argument is that the copy from which *Two Gentlemen* was printed in the First Folio was itself a copy from a manuscript which had the acts already marked in it, and that consequently this division is unlikely to be original, but an insert into prompt-copy. This assumption, however, is certainly contrary to the pertinent surviving facts, where the authors inserted and the actors ejected. And as to the massed headings, they have been applied to Webster's *Duchess of Malfy,* with the author vouching for the originality of his work, whether from foul paper or fair. It would seem that massed headings could get applied to any available type of manuscript, author's uncut original, cut copy, what not. That follows from its editorial origin, whether for literary or for stage purposes. I do not see, therefore, how these characteristics can indicate that the copy for *Two Gentlemen* was from prompt-copy rather than from some form more directly descended from the author's own manuscript.

This was, at least once upon a time, the opinion of Professor Bald. With his attention fixed principally upon Webster's *Duchess of Malfy,* he wrote, "with the exceedingly doubtful exception of the stage direction at IV. ii. 165–7 of *The Dutchesse of Malfy,* there is nothing in these texts to suggest that any of the manuscripts from which they were printed was intended for use in the theatre or had ever been used there; on the contrary, the very form of the texts seems definitely to show a disregard of theatrical conditions."[18] This "classical" characteristic could have been applied to any type of text, but it remains to distinguish the type in *Two Gentlemen.*

This assumption that Shakspere did not write in acts will necessitate readjustment in numerous places. But two further instances from Sir Walter must suffice for the present. For *Errors,* "An unoriginal division into acts only has been intro-

18 R. C. Bald, "'Assembled' Texts," 4 *Library,* XII, 247.

duced, perhaps at the time of printing, since the unusual direction at V. i. 10, 'Enter Antipholus and Dromio againe,' after
their exit at the end of Act IV, shows that the action was meant
to be continuous."[19]

Whatever else this jotting may be, it is initially the
author's "rough" identification of characters, and belongs to the
sequence of such identifications for which this play is notorious.[20]
In the final section of the preceding act, this set of twins had
been identified at entrance as "Enter Antipholus Siracusia with
his Rapier drawne, and Dromio Sirac." At the end of the act,
we have "Exeunt." Then after the first nine lines of the next
act, "Enter Antipholus and Dromio againe." The "againe"
merely identifies which set is entering here. It is not properly a
stage-direction at all. And even if the "againe" was inserted by
anyone other than the author, it is still only for identification.
This set of twins had gone out; and it was this same set, not the
other as one might expect, which was coming on again. The same
set was coming on again, after only nine lines out, even if there
had also been a curtain between, as on that stage there had not
been. There is mental continuity here on the part of the author
or of some annotator, but no necessary indication of stage
continuity.

But even if this had been a stage-direction indicating continuous action, that fact, if established, would still have no bearing on the question of the original structure of the play. If there
is one thing which can be demonstrated beyond doubt for
Errors, it is the fact that it was constructed in five units, and
that those units are properly marked in the First Folio.[21] The
play is so mechanically constructed that there cannot possibly
be doubt in the face of any competent analysis of its technical
composition. The play was constructed in acts, but that fact has

19 Greg, *First Folio,* p. 201.
20 See below, pp. 84 ff.
21 See my analysis, among others, in the edition of 1928, before I had located any statement of the five-act formula, and in *Five-Act,* pp. 704ff.

no bearing on the question of whether its act-divisions were observed upon the stage.

An analogous instance occurs in *Dream,* where in the First Folio "They sleepe all the Act." Says Sir Walter, "This was clearly not original, for one of the divisions has been made at a point where the lovers are asleep on the stage . . . This presumably means both that the division was made in the theatre and not merely for printing, and that the intervals were of some duration, probably with music."[22] In the purely mathematical sequence of, "Drop, drop, who has the drop?" the two couples have been carefully and purposefully worked into position and put to sleep on the stage at the end of the main sequence—"Two of both kinds make four" (438)—ready to be waked into the final correct combination of two and two; that is, this is unquestionably an act-division.[23] The problem for staging was whether to wake the couples, get them off the stage, and then bring them back and put them to sleep again for the final stage of their complications, or simply to let them sleep till wanted. The decision was to let them "sleepe all the Act," including the act-division.

The couples, being now at the end of their involution, are forced by the mathematical structure of the plot to sleep through the greater part of the next act till in the evolution of the sequence their turn comes. Since Titania is the key figure, she must lead the way in the evolution. So she and Bottom are next put to sleep at the beginning of the fourth act, in order that Titania may be immediately awakened into concord, while the two earthly couples and Bottom, under the admonition "Sleepers Lye still," wait their turn, with Bottom's "cue" arousing him last of all, his head still full of *Bottomes Dreame* as he joins his fellow mechanicals to end the act. The couples

22 Greg, *First Folio,* pp. 243–44.
23 See Baldwin, *Five-Act,* p. 479; and the full analysis in *On the Literary Genetics of Shakspere's Plays, 1592–1594,* Chapter XXVIII.

had slept not only through the act-division but also through most of the sequent act, as directed: "They sleepe all the Act."[24]

From such an instance as in *Errors* we cannot argue either that the play was not written in acts or that the act-divisions were or were not observed upon the stage. In the case of *Dream,* the whole point was how on the stage to bridge not only an awkward act-division, but also for their stage an awkward act. Acts and act-divisions are two quite distinct things, and past scholarship has a great deal of untangling to do here, though for the present the above instances must serve.

But to return now to Wilson's theory of assembled texts, he turns next to scenes, which elicit his special theory of assembled texts. "It is difficult to conceive any theatrical necessity for the insertion of scenes into a prompt-copy, but there was theatrical material which, if furnished with such prompt-copy, would render the introduction of scene-divisions into a printed text a very easy matter, though they might not, and in the Folio often do not, correspond with a modern editor's sense of literary or dramatic fitness. This theatrical material was the manuscript 'plot' of the play, which gave the entries and exits of the actors, and across which a line was drawn when the stage was left empty by one group of players to make room for another. With 'copy' in which the acts were marked, and with the 'plot' on which the 'exeunt omnes' lines were ruled, scene-division would present no difficulty to Jaggard."[25] It is true, as we have seen, that the scene is the basic and only unit for theatrical plots, even if it can be considered to be a unit. But there is no evidence that theatrical plots were ever made for Shakspere's plays, or that for the First Folio Jaggard, of all persons, or anyone else would need to turn to such a theatrical plot, or that actually

24 Apparently some would interpret "Act" here to mean act-division. But *NED* cites no instance where act means act-division, and I know of none. Titania had similarly and for similar reasons bridged the act-division between the second and third acts with a long nap in her "flowery bed" till Bottom could be moved into position for her awaking into infatuation.

anyone in this period ever did so turn to reconstruct a play for any purpose. And the characteristics which have elicited these theories of assembled texts belonged definitely to a known contemporary type, to be found among other places in the hundreds of editions of Terence, compulsorily known to every grammar school boy of ten or so. Judging by the dozens of editions of Terence which I own and the hundreds I have seen, I think it is safe to say that no edition of Shakspere's day marked either entrance or exit. They did not need to. Typically they have simply the formal act and scene heading, with all the characters of the scene grouped together beneath. In Plautus, the acts are usually numbered, and occasionally the scenes. But, of course, the actors are grouped under the heading for each change, as in Terence. The custom of writing "Enter" and "Exit" did not come from the texts of the classics, though it does trace from the Latin tradition (see *NED*). In view of the custom in classical plays, surely we need not trouble further about theories of "assembled texts" which are based on the "classical" characteristic.

But the units and the consequent divisions are perfectly clear.

25 *Tempest,* ed. Quiller-Couch & Wilson (1921), pp. xxxvi–xxxvii. Wilson eventually adds *As You Like It* and *Merchant of Venice* to the five of Rhodes; three is the limit. Wilson has now come over to "foul papers," at least for *Errors* (ed. 1962, p. 65).

Chapter Five

COMEDIES WITH ACTS ONLY

IN THE FIRST FOLIO

WE HAVE NOW considered the seven comedies of the first class in the First Folio; those with acts and scenes. The remaining seven comedies belong predominantly to our second class, showing only act-division, as is characteristic of one type of surviving copy made specifically for the stage. Following the first four comedies, which are of the first class, we have five of the second class, consisting of *Errors,* followed by four plays with "good" quarto forbears (*Ado, Labour's, Dream, Merchant*). Incidentally, the grouping itself shows that those responsible were actively aware of the quartos as a group, as, of course, they would be physically aware because of the different and uniform format, if the quartos were physically present. The grouping is in turn a strong argument that the quartos were used in some physical capacity.[1] *Errors* is in acts only, though as Capell says, its scenes are normal. The four previously printed plays which follow *Errors* in the First Folio are now in acts, though in the previous quartos neither act nor scene had been indicated. For these four, the compositors of the First Folio necessarily had some manuscript authority for the act-headings.

In all instances, the compositors must have had con-

---

1 In several cases, Jonson used copies of early quartos upon which to correct, supplement, etc. the text for his Folio of 1616 (See Greg's summaries in his *Bibliography,* Vol. I). Under the conditions, that was the common-sense procedure.

siderably more from manuscript than these act-headings. According to Sir Walter Greg, in the First Folio *Ado* was "Printed from a copy of [Q] containing some playhouse notes and corrections."[2] *Labour's* was "Printed from [Q] with some alterations."[3] *Dream* was "Printed from a copy of [the false Q] containing some prompter's annotations."[4] *Merchant* was "Printed from a copy of [the true Quarto] containing a few playhouse notes and alterations."[5] Thus for the comedies the First Folio is supposed in every possible case to have used a preceding quarto.[6] In the two cases where there was choice, the selectors used the true quarto in one instance and the false reprint in the other. As a matter of fact, they seem still in the case of *Merchant* to stand accused of having made some use of the false reprint as well as of the true original. Professor J. Dover Wilson submitted a half-dozen uneasy connections with this quarto of 1619 to Sir Walter Greg, who "thinks it 'most unlikely that in 1619 Jaggard should have had any access to playhouse MSS.' His tentative suggestion is that the copy of Q. 1600 (revised) from which Q. 1619 was printed may have been 'still in Jaggard's office in 1623' [the date would be by or before 1622, which would make the suggestion more plausible] and have undergone 'further revision by collation with the playhouse copy and was then used as copy for F'."[7] According

2 Greg, *Bibliography,* I, 275. Sir Walter has more detailed statements on all these plays in his *Folio,* with some variations; but for our purposes the succinct summaries in the *Bibliography* will serve, and I have usually simply quoted, so as to have the considered and consistent opinion of our fullest authority, without indicating whether I agree, unless agreement or disagreement has some fundamental bearing on the main problem.

3 Greg, *Bibliography,* I, 245.

4 Greg, *Bibliography,* I, 277.

5 Greg, *Bibliography,* I, 279.

6 "The quartos of *Love's Labour's Lost* and *Romeo and Juliet* were reprinted almost as they stood . . . in the case of *Much Ado, A Midsummer-Night's Dream,* and *The Merchant of Venice* some reference was made to the prompt-book in the matter of stage directions" (Greg, *Folio,* p. 429). The fundamental fact is that manuscript was involved with nearly, and probably all, the plays which had previously been printed in quarto, and that the manuscripts used were of the types we have distinguished among surviving manuscripts. For present

to the accounts of the experts, then there was no discrimination between the "good" good quartos and the false reprints of "good" quartos. At best, or worst, those responsible simply assembled a set of "good" quartos upon which to make copies for the Folio. In 1619, the printers and publishers had not discriminated even between "good" and "bad." But now the call was at least for "good" quartos, and it was evidently met by the most readily available, catch as catch can. However attractive the idea that the actors had each time procured a copy of the latest edition to serve as a prompt-copy and that this was turned over for print, it cannot be upheld as the rule, even though Pope instanced a copy (perhaps of *Romeo and Juliet?*) similarly marked, but when and by whom he does not say.[8]

Wilson would have all four of these fortuitously selected quartos checked to playhouse manuscript. But Greg thinks that in the case of *Labour's* "There is indeed nothing whatever to connect F with the playhouse or to suggest that the few alterations it contains were anything but editorial."[9] But in any case the editor had to consult eventually some manuscript in order to restore the acts, and that manuscript would under the conditions necessarily be some form of manuscript destined for the theater. If we may judge by the poor job the "editor" did upon the act-headings,[10] the manuscript consulted was no improvement over the one, if different, which underlies the quarto.

purposes, it makes no difference whether quartos were used in the transmission from manuscript to folio. I have, therefore, used Greg's authoritative summaries, without any implication whether the quartos were or were not used in the transmission, and without any attempt to supplement Greg's conclusions, pro or con, past or present. Nor, consequently, shall I "protest" every time I use such statements.

7 *Merchant,* ed. Quiller-Couch & Wilson (1926), pp. 176–77 *n.*

8 "I have seen one [quarto] in particu-

lar (which seems to have belonged to the playhouse, by having the parts divided with lines, and the Actors names in the margin) where several of those very passages were added in a written hand, which are since to be found in the folio" (Pope, *Shakespear* (1725), I, xvii). My colleague, Professor G. B. Evans, tells me he has not come upon this copy in his ransacking for early print used as prompt.

9 W. W. Greg, *Editorial Problem in Shakespeare,* p. 128.

10 Baldwin, *Five-Act,* pp. 579ff.

All indications are that available manuscript for this play in 1621, as in 1598, was something of a mess.

If in each of these four cases the compositors were following a printed quarto with manuscript additions, as present opinion holds (I do not need to express an opinion), then these act-divisions were in some way indicated in manuscript. If the compositors were not reproducing printed quartos to this extent edited, then they were following directly manuscripts of the second class or copies of that form. In either case, the authority consists of manuscripts of the second class. The quartos originally had been printed from undivided copies of prompt-books. If we accept prevailing theory, they were now checked to prompt-book copies but divided as to acts. The quartos have thus been checked to their corresponding type, if not to the same manuscripts. Since the checked quartos were supposed to stand in lieu of manuscripts of this type, *Errors,* which was the same type of manuscript, was put into the same batch with the corrected quartos, whether accidentally or purposely, thus forming this second group of five plays. If the quartos were not used for transmission of the manuscript text, then five plays were submitted together in manuscripts with acts marked, four of which had already been printed in quarto without acts marked, the four being grouped together, following the one play, *Errors,* directly from manuscript. At any rate, the type of manuscript being reproduced caused the grouping of these five plays, whether the four quartos were used or not as agents for transmitting the manuscripts of their plays. Since it was not a matter of "editorial policy" to insert act-divisions in all plays, one may wonder why this feature should be inserted in the quartos.

In fact, Wilson has been struck by the relationship of *Errors,* to the four plays with quarto background. "There are certain features of the text [of *Errors*] which might tempt one

11 *Comedy,* ed. Wilson (1922, 1962), p. 65.

to believe that the Folio printers had here a lost Quarto to go upon, as they had Quartos, not lost, in the case of the succeeding four plays in the volume. . . . Yet it exhibits phenomena which mark it off as different not only from any Folio text we have hitherto handled but also from the Good Quartos as a class."[11] As a manuscript, *Errors* was naturally placed to follow the four copied manuscripts of the first class, and to be followed by the four quartos checked to manuscript of the second class.

Besides *Errors,* there are two other plays of the second class from manuscript, *Shrew* and *Well.* These two connect with a sub-group of the second type by preserving the names of a few minor actors, showing that they were directly from stage copy, if they were not themselves stage copy.[12] Of the quartos for the comedies, *Ado* had been printed with such names, and picked up more when supposedly its quarto was checked to manuscript for the First Folio, while similarly the quarto of *Dream* also picked up such notations from the manuscript to which it had been checked. One would have expected *Shrew* and *Well* to be placed with *Comedy* before the quartos, or to follow them directly, but for some reason *Like It* of the first class gets inserted between them and the quartos. It is rather curious, though probably not significant, that *Like It* should have been placed next to the quarto copies, since the play had itself so narrowly escaped becoming a "good" quarto in 1600. Had it been so printed it would doubtless have been checked for the First Folio to manuscripts of the second class, as had they. Presumably also the manuscript from which it was proposed to print it in 1600 would not have returned to the company, and this could have been the cause that *Like It* was printed from a manuscript of the first class. Except for the interruption by *Like It,* all plays of the second class are grouped together, with *Night* of the first class to end the comedies, and the copied *Tale* of the first class being added later.

12 See below, pp. 84 ff.

The procedure of those who directed the preparation of the copies to be used by the printers of the First Folio is now reasonably clear. Not later than 1621, they set the professional copyist Ralph Crane to copying certainly four plays, and probably five. Four of these (*Tempest, Gentlemen, Wives, Measure*) they sent to the printers, who began actual printing about February 1, 1622. The fifth, *Tale,* apparently because of classification, they retained, but finally decided to attach it at the end of the comedies. All five of these plays marked acts and scenes, indicating descent from author's autograph, though most, if not all five, were only copies of copies. They next turned to plays of the second class, furnishing a manuscript of *Errors* (second-class) to follow the four manuscripts of the first-class. Then came in succession all four of the comedies which had been printed in quarto (*Ado, Labour's, Dream, Merchant*), but checked in each case to a manuscript of the second class, so that the quartos were merely agents of transmission for these manuscripts. Next came three manuscripts (*Like It, Shrew, Well*). *Shrew,* and *Well* were copies, or copies of copies, which had seen some actual service as acting copies. *Like It* of the first class probably got attached to these to form a group of three manuscripts, to follow the group of four quartos. It and *Night* had evidently come to light after the first group of copies was made, though so far the evidence we have been considering has not indicated that *Like It* was a copy. To continue this final mopping up operation, the copied *Night* was attached, and eventually the copied copy *Tale* rounded off the whole.

So seven of the ten plays from manuscript are of the first class. Six, and probably all seven, were special copies, five of them by Crane. Clearly, manuscript of the first class had here been preferred for copies. The other three manuscripts were of the second class, apparently not special copies. The four quartos were checked to manuscripts of the second class. These quartos were printed originally from undivided stage-copies and were now checked about 1622 also to stage-copies, which at this period would likely have the acts indicated in the margin, if not in the text. These could, of course, be the same stage-copies from which the quartos were originally descended. This method of checking would involve a minimum of "correction," since the autographs would doubtless have presented more variants, especially in detail.

Quite clearly, the choices generally have been a matter of convenience. The seven plays from manuscripts of the first class preserve the acts and scenes marked, as in the usual author's autograph. Three other manuscripts have only the acts, as is characteristic of one kind of manuscript for the stage, and the four quartos have been checked to this type. The eventual score is even, seven of the first class, and seven of the second. Where full copies had to be made, they were made from manuscripts of the first class, with the proper authorial stigmata, though probably in all instances these were only copies of copies, sometimes already adapted, not even of Shakspere's autograph. The other seven were the most convenient forms available from copies of the second class, to some extent adapted to the stage. There is no sign of any urgent intent to reproduce Shakspere's actual autograph in detail. They simply procured, by the easiest methods they could think of, what they considered to be sufficiently authentic copies for printing. The resultant happy hunting ground should keep bibliographers busy for the foreseeable future.

Chapter Six

IRREGULAR SPEECH HEADINGS

THE THEORY of "assembled texts" has also been bolstered by irregular speech-headings. It will thus be well to see if there is any correlation of this characteristic with our two classes of "Prompt-Books." In his edition of *The Comedy of Errors* (1922), Professor J. Dover Wilson used "Speech-headings and stage-directions" to argue that *Errors* is an assembled text. "Assuming then that the copy for *The Comedy of Errors*, 1623, was not Shakespeare's original but some sort of transcript therefrom, written in the playhouse at dictation, we have next to enquire what was the character of this transcript and for what purpose was it made? The question introduces us to a consideration of the most patent peculiarity of the text, its strange stage-directions. But before dealing with these we shall do well to look at the speech-headings.

"In the Good Quartos, as we shall find, Shakespeare was both careless and forgetful in regard to the names of his minor characters, such carelessness generally denoting revision of an old text. In *Errors* the word 'Egeon' occurs five times in the dialogue . . . but never in the speech-headings or the stage-directions. At the head of 1. 1. he is described as 'the Merchant of Siracusa,' and his speeches in this scene are labelled with various abbreviations of 'Merchant.' But the play is full of 'merchants,' and in 5. 1. matters become complicated, since there

is another merchant (name unknown) also present. Aegeon's
first speech in 5. 1. is therefore headed 'Mar. Fat.' (i.e. merchant father) and the others 'Fa.,' 'Fath.,' 'Fat.' and so on. Yet
the use of 'Eg.' would seem to have offered a far less clumsy
way out of the difficulty. Why was it not resorted to? The right
answer may be that Shakespeare was revising an old play, and
could not be bothered to remember the name 'Egeon,' except
when it cropped up in the dialogue he was working upon. . . .
In the same way, though the speech-heading 'Ang.' is employed
for Angelo in 3. 1. and 3. 2., he becomes 'Gold.' (i.e. goldsmith) for the rest of the play.

"On the other hand, there are speech-headings which we
cannot attribute to Shakespeare, since they were undoubtedly
added after the transcript was made. Indeed we can be tolerably
certain that the bulk of the speech-headings were written by one
scribe and the bulk of the stage-directions by another, who
occasionally altered the speech-headings."[1]

"The conclusion we draw from all this is that the 'copy'
which reached the printers in 1623 was composite in character,
the dialogue and a few brief stage-directions being in Hand A,
and that Hand B, after the dictated transcript was finished,
went over the whole thing filling out the stage-directions and
in places touching up the speech-headings. We shall find further
evidence in support of this conclusion as we proceed to examine
the stage-directions more minutely."[2]

1 *Comedy,* ed. Quiller-Couch and Wilson (1922), pp. 68–69.
2 *Ibid.,* p. 71.
3 *Ibid.,* pp. 72–73. Functionally, these
stage-directions are not duplications
at all; the characters evidently leave
in two groups, and so require two
stage-directions. After Adriana has
promised the Officer to assume her
husband's debt and has put the latter
in Pinch's charge, she says
    Go beare him hence,
        sister go you with me
It was thus clearly intended that
Adriana and Luciana should keep together. As that group goes out,
Adriana, with Luciana, turns to the
Officer and the Courtezan to get information about her husband's alleged debts. When Antipholus of
Syracuse and his Dromio rush in with
rapiers drawn, Adriana says, "Let's
call more helpe to haue them bound
againe," and the stage-direction is
"Runne all out." The Officer is a bit
slower to recognize the danger;
Antipholus was not "mad" at him;

"We have already seen indications that two hands had been at work upon the stage-directions. Perhaps the most glaring instance of the kind is the direction quoted above from 4.4. 145, 'Runne all out'/'Exeunt omnes, as fast as may be, frighted.' Commenting on this in his recent book, *The Stagery of Shakespeare,* Mr. Crompton Rhodes writes: 'It is safe to say that the prompt-book had merely 'Exeunt omnes,' the additions being made for reasons external and literary, and not internal and theatrical." . . . We agree that 'Exeunt omnes' probably stood first in the text and that the rest was added later. . . . But, as we have just seen, there is nothing necessarily untheatrical about this addition, while the duplication of stage-directions by different scribes is very common in prompt-copy. There are, for example, three or four instances of it in the MS of *Sir Thomas More.* Clearly 'Exeunt omnes' was in Hand A, and 'Runne all out, as fast as may be, frighted' in Hand B, who was revising the stage-directions for theatrical purposes."[3]

"Our theory then is that the copy for *The Comedy of Errors,* 1623, was a dictated transcript, made in the playhouse sometime in the early 'nineties, and prepared for the stage by elaborate stage-directions from the hand of an actor with vivid memories of the old *Historie of Error.* But if so, why was the addition of these stage-directions necessary, and why in the process did they take this elaborate form? We can discover only one satisfactory answer to the first of these questions. If the

but seeing the determined two advancing with rapiers drawn, he shouts, "Away, they'l kill vs," and rushes off, doubtless with the Courtezan in chase, the stage-direction being, "Exeunt omnes, as fast as may be, frighted." Being ladies, Adriana and Luciana get the more dignified exeunt. But the Officer and the Courtezan were evidently expected to do full justice to the comic possibilities in their flight "as fast as may be, frighted." One wonders how voluminous and varicolored were the Courtezan's skirts, and how she managed with them! The duplication of the exeunt, such as it is, lies in situation and phraseology, not in function. Both stage-directions are required functionally, and there is no evidence that they have been scrambled phraseologically. "Exeunt omnes" is the colorless and conventional stage direction, of course, to which further descriptive addition has been made, but not necessarily by a different person.

transcriber, Hand A, had been working direct from Shake-speare's MS, which would be the prompt-copy, the stage-directions of this original (for it must have contained adequate stage-directions) would naturally have been dictated to him with the dialogue. Since, however, the bulk of the stage-directions were patently added after the transcription had been made, we infer that the transcript was based not upon the prompt-copy but upon players' parts, in which stage-directions would be quite inadequate or non-existent. Yet we believe, as stated above, that the transcriber was able to insert a few brief stage-directions as he proceeded with his task, and we account for their presence by supposing that the theatrical 'plot' was available at the time for consultation."[4]

The whole argument here rests upon inconsistencies. As I stated in 1928, "The general method of the New Cambridge editors . . . is to discover inconsistencies in the play, to group these together in more or less harmonious aggregations, and then to assume that each of these groups represents a stage in the development of the play. But inconsistencies in Shakespeare do not necessarily prove divided authorship. Every play of Shakespeare's, as scholars have for generations carved them-selves reputations by showing, is filled with more or less serious inconsistencies of characterization, time scheme, stated facts, spelling, punctuation, the weather, and what not."[5]

"Another seemingly certain point is that either the final scribe of *The Comedy,* whether Shakespeare or another, or the compositor who set up the text, was also hopelessly inconsistent in such matters of form as the abbreviations for names attached to speeches, and in other small details. Since the text is re-markably good throughout, we may free the compositor from blame, and may also be certain that the final scribe had pre-sented at least a clear, if not a minutely consistent, manuscript.

"As illustration of this inconsistency of form for names, in

4 *Ibid,* pp. 74-75.

Act. I, we find Duke of Ephesus, Duk, Duke; Merchant of Siracusa, Mer, Merch; Marchant, E. Mar.; Antipholis Erotes, Ant; Dromio, Dro; Dromio of Ephesus, E. Dro., Dromio Ep. In Act II, Adriana, wife to Antipholus Sereptus, Adr, Adri, Ad; Luciana, Luc, Luci; Antipholis Errotis, Ant, E Ant, Antiph, Anti, An, Antip; Dromio Eph, E Dro, E Dr, Dro; Dromio Siracusia, S Dro, S Dr, Drom. In Act III, Antipholus of Ephesus, E Anti, E Ant, E An, Anti, Ant; Antipholus of Siracusia, S Anti, Ant, Anti; Dromio, E Dro, E Drom; Dromio, S Dro, Dromio Siracusia, Dro; Angelo, Ang; Balthaser, Bal, Baltz, Balth; Luce; Adriana, Adri, Adr; Iuliana, Iulia, Luc. In Act IV, Antipholus Ephes, Ant, Eph Ant, Anti, An; Antipholus Siracusia, Ant, S. Ant; Dromio, Dro, S Dro, S Dromio, Dromio Sir, Dromio Sirac; Adriana, Adr, Adria, Adri; Luciana, Luc, Luci; Curtizan, Cur, Courtizan, Curt; Officer, Offi, Offic, Off; Merchant, Mar; Goldsmith, Gold; Pinch. In Act V, Antipholus Siracusa, Antipholus, Ant, S Ant; Antipholus, E Ant, E Anti, E An; Dromio, S Dro, Dromio Sir; E Dromio of Ephesus, E Dro, Dro, E. D; Adriana, Adr, Adri, Ad; Luciana, Luc; Courtezan, Cur, Curt; Abbesse, Ab, Abb; Duke of Ephesus, Duke; Merchant of Siracusa, Mar Fat, Fa, Fath; Goldsmith, Gold; Merchant, Mar; Messenger, Mess.

"Here is no sign of any attempt at consistency in name forms, but a higgledy-piggledy welter, to be worked out only by the law of permutations and combinations. These variants, too, are so scattered and so intermingled throughout the play that they cannot be accounted for by supposing that they are the result of different authors, scribes, or compositors. We can hardly find a dozen speeches together without several of these variants. Yet with all the variants and inconsistent practice, there is no doubt or confusion in even a single case as to which character was being referred to. That was the only consistency which had any practical value to Shakespeare and his company;

5 *Errors,* ed. T. W. Baldwin (1928), p. 101.

that consistency they observed. Inconsistency in other matters is thus of highly dubious value for proving divided workmanship on the play. The fundamental difficulty with the method of inconsistencies is that it proves too much."[6]

In a work written mostly in 1931–32, but not published till 1947, I restated in more detail my earlier summary for the double twins. "The fact that these forms belong only to the first two acts suggests that those may in some way be different from the latter three, in which there is change. It will thus be well to watch these names evolve through the play. The first of the twins to appear is 'Antipholis Erotes,' the name being abbreviated consistently 'Ant.' With him appears his Dromio, who in his only speech is designated 'Dro.' Then 'Exit Dromio.' Next, 'Dromio of Ephesus' enters and is consistently designated 'E. Dro.' till he exits as 'Dromio Ep.' At the beginning of the second act, 'Enter Adriana, wife to Antipholis Sereptus.' Then 'Enter Dromio Eph.,' who begins as 'E. Dro.,' becomes 'E. Dr.,' and then just 'Dro.,' as there was no necessity of further distinction as to which Dromio was involved. Next 'Enter Antipholis Errotis,' and to him shortly 'Enter Dromio Siracusia.' Then 'E. Ant.' becomes 'Ant.,' 'Antip.,' 'Antiph.,' or 'An.' without further distinction, but Dromio retains his 'S.'

"Then the 'significant' designations of the twin masters are leveled to the place names which the twin servants had borne from the beginning. This was doubtless to avoid confusion, since under the system of the first two acts the 'E' servant was attached to the 'S' master, and vice versa. Now that the second twin master was to appear and that both sets of twins are to be brought into juxtaposition, it was not desirable to confound confusion with this further complication. So the twin masters are now leveled to the place names, which the twin servants had borne from the beginning, as the easier to grasp and remember, instead of the 'significant' ones they had inherited. But since no

6 *Ibid.*, pp. 102–103.

confusion was possible in the first two acts, the horses were swapped in mid-stream, without the trouble of returning to the bank of the beginning.

"So at the beginning of the third act 'Enter Antipholus of Ephesus,' who has his 'E' for a few speeches, but soon drops it, though his Dromio keeps his 'E,' since the other Dromio is quite active on the other side of the closed door, and consequently has his 'S' for distinction. It is now the turn of 'Antipholus of Siracusia' to take the stage, as he of Ephesus leaves. He has the 'S' to his first speech, but thereafter it is dropped. Similarly, 'Enter Dromio, Siracusia,' who has an 'S' to his first speech, but not thereafter. In the fourth act, 'Enter Antipholus Ephes.,' who has no distinction to his first speech, but 'Eph. Ant.' to his second, and none thereafter. His Dromio is designated only as 'Dro.' in his one speech, though 'Enter Dromio Sira.,' who is in his first speech 'Dro.,' but thereafter gets the 'S.' Next 'Enter S. Dromio,' who is 'Dro.' in his first speech, but then gets the 'S' throughout. Then 'Enter Antipholus Siracusia,' who gets no 'S,' but 'Enter Dromio Sir.,' who gets 'S' throughout. Similarly, 'Enter Antipholus Ephes.,' who gets no 'E,' but 'Enter Dromio Eph.,' who gets his 'E' for several speeches but finally loses it. Finally, 'Enter Antipholus Siracusia . . . and Dromio Sirac,' each of whom gets an 'S' in his first speech, but not thereafter. So when they reappear immediately in the fifth act, 'Enter Antipholus and Dromio againe,' and neither gets an 'S' till Dromio's final speech. Finally, 'Enter Antipholus and E. Dromio of Ephesus.' Since they are about to be confronted with the opposite pair they regularly, though not quite always get their 'E' as the other set gets its 'S,' to the end of the play.

"The reader will notice the curious and seamless evolution by which when the twin masters were finally opposed in the third act it was decided to designate them by their cities as the servants had been from the beginning. Otherwise, an 'E' master would have been paired with an 'S' servant. So the system began theoretically, with 'significant' names for the twin-masters as had been true in the source; but at the pragmatic point leveled to practicality, though it found no reason to revise to uniformity. Similarly, there is the evident habitual tendency to distinguish a twin character by significant letter for the first speech or so, and not thereafter, unless both of a pair are in proximity, when constant distinction is needed. But again this tendency has not been standardized to consistency. These habitual tendencies evidently represent one mind as it worked its problem through, but a mind that cared for consistency no whit further than clarity of identification demanded. Clearly, too, this is the mind of the composer, not that of a scribe. Further, the entrance headings for the twin masters were put in originally by the composer himself, not by a scribe of any type, since they originate from the source plays. In other words, here is William Shakspere himself at work, though the actual manuscript used by the compositor was not necessarily Shakspere's autograph."[7]

Dr. McKerrow[8] in 1933 pursued a similar line of thinking. "First as regards the characters. It is well known that in the early texts of many of the plays characters appear under different names in different parts of the play. Thus in the *Comedy of Errors* the father of the brothers Antipholus is in the text named Aegeon, but in none of the stage directions, nor in the speakers' names, does 'Aegeon' appear. Instead he is variously described, as 'Merchant of Syracuse,' 'Merchant,' 'Merchant Father,' and simply 'Father.' This does not, I think, imply that the stage directions and speakers' names were added by some 'editor' but merely that the author, to whom Aegeon was a clear-cut and distinct personality, was in each case thinking of the function which at the moment he performed in the action of the play, and instinctively, and naturally, gave him the designa-

7 Baldwin, *Five-Act,* pp. 698–700.
8 I sent Dr. McKerrow a copy of my

work of 1928, which he acknowledged graciously and helpfully, as was his

tion which this function called for. To the reader, however, these changes are disconcerting, and we may be thankful to Rowe that in his edition 'Aegeon' is 'Aegeon' wherever he appears, and that in the same play the person who is in the folios sometimes 'Angelo' and sometimes 'Goldsmith' has become 'Angelo' throughout."[9]

Dr. McKerrow later proceeded to make an examination of this characteristic of consistent or inconsistent speech-headings for all the plays. In *Two Gentlemen* as representative of one type of printed play "the names given to the characters are permanent labels, and are quite unaffected by the function of the character at the moment. This of course accords with the practice followed in printing plays nowadays, whether these are modern or ancient.

"When, however, we turn to the *Comedy of Errors* we find a very different state of affairs. The names by which the characters are indicated, instead of being the same throughout, frequently depend, much as they do in a novel, on the progress of the story or on the person with whom the character is conversing. Thus the father of the two brothers Antipholus, whom we know from the text to be named Egeon, is in the opening stage-direction described '*Merchant of Siracusa*,' and throughout the first scene is, as a speaker, simply *Merchant*. In the next scene, however, a different merchant (of Ephesus) appears, and later, in IV. 1., another. Both these characters are called as speakers simply 'Merchant' (*Mar., E. Mar., Mer.*). In V. 1., however, while this last Merchant is on the stage Egeon enters and recognizes his sons. As his original designation of 'Merchant' is now in use for someone else, Egeon becomes first 'Merchant Father' (*Mar. Fat.*) and later simply 'Father.'

"Similarly the goldsmith Angelo is called 'Angelo' at his

9 R. B. McKerrow, *The Treatment of* / *Shakespeare's Text by His Earlier Editors 1709–1768*, p. 11.

first entry in III. i. and again in III. ii. Later, however, his business as a goldsmith being the chief point of his existence in the play, he is, as a speaker, simply 'Goldsmith,' and so for the rest of the play, his personal name Angelo being dropped.

"More significant than either of these, but also more complicated, is the case of the brothers Antipholus and the two Dromios. The first of the four to appear is Antipholus of Syracuse, called at his entrance '*Antipholus Erotes*' (actually he is here and in some other places called 'Antipholis'. I ignore these minor variations or misprints, as also 'Errotis' in II. ii. for 'Erotes'), whose name, as a speaker, is abbreviated simply to '*Ant.*,' his servant Dromio being '*Dro.*' When, shortly after, the second Dromio enters, this latter is, in order to distinguish the two, called '*Dromio of Ephesus*,' abbreviated to '*E. Dro.*'

"There is now (II. ii) a re-entry of Antipholus of Syracuse, who is still called 'Antipholus Erotes,' his second speech being marked '*E. Ant.*,' the later ones simply '*Ant.*' as before; but the first Dromio, returning, is now '*Dromio Siracusia*' (*S. Dro.*). We thus have the confusing arrangement of the master being called '*E. Ant.*' or simply '*Ant.*,' while his servant is '*S. Dro.*'

"At the beginning of Act III. the other Antipholus enters for the first time. He is '*Antipholus of Ephesus*,' abbreviated to '*E. Anti.*,' or '*E. An.*,' the distinctions of '*E. Dro.*,' and '*S. Dro.*' being maintained. When in III. ii. Antipholus of Syracuse reappears, the confusing '*Antipholus Erotes*' (*E. Ant.*) is dropped and his name is on the first occasion given as '*S. Anti.*' but for the rest of the scene merely '*Ant.*' or '*Anti.*' Similarly in IV. i. his brother, who enters as '*Antipholus Ephes.*' appears in the speech-headings once as '*Eph. Ant.*' but elsewhere as '*Anti.*' or '*Ant.*' From this point onwards the four are consistently distinguished as '*E. Ant.*,' '*S. Ant.*,' '*E. Dro.*,' and '*S. Dro.*'

10 R. B. McKerrow, "A Suggestion Regarding Shakespeare's Manuscripts," *RES*, XI (1935), pp. 460–64.

"To put it briefly, the writer of the MS. evidently marked the distinctions between the two pairs of characters only as and when this became necessary. Further we can see that he had not considered in advance how he could best do this, for having determined to call Dromio of Ephesus '*E. Dro.*' he indicates Antipholus Erotes (the Syracusan), when he needs to distinguish him from his brother, by '*E. Ant.*' Later, however, it becomes obvious that the E. and S. of the Antipholi should correspond with the E. and S. of the Dromios, and he calls Antipholus Surreptus (of Ephesus) '*E. Ant.*' and Erotes '*S. Ant.*,' dropping in fact the confusing 'Surreptus' and 'Erotes' altogether."[10]

Dr. McKerrow then works out the opposing classes of regulars and irregulars. For the comedies, he groups four plays (*Gentlemen, Measure, Shrew, Night*) as having consistent speech-headings. These are all plays of the first class except *Shrew*, where Sir Walter Greg says, "we must except the Induction,"[11] and Capell classes the play as a whole as irregular. Thus three out of the seven of the first class are regular. Of the three, only one (*Gentlemen*) has the "classical" characteristic, but two are supposed to be Crane copies, his other three copies being neither notably good nor bad in this respect. The other four of the first class (*Tempest, Wives, Like It, Tale*) are not characterized by Dr. McKerrow, therefore are presumably neither notably regular nor irregular in their speech-headings. At any rate, only four of the fourteen comedies are notably consistent in their speech-headings, and three of these four belonged to the seven regular plays of the first class, two of the three being Crane copies. Consistent speech-headings are not characteristic of Shakspere's comedies, and appear in less than half of even those of the first class.

On the other hand, Dr. McKerrow groups *Errors, Labour's, Dream, Merchant* (where Sir Walter Greg says "the

11 Greg, *First Folio*, p. 113 n.

feature is less marked"[12]), and *Well* as having notably inconsistent speech-headings, these being five of the seven plays
of the second class. Three of the five had "good" quarto forbears, which had not been regularized (*Labour's, Dream,
Merchant*), and were themselves not regularized in this respect
for the First Folio. The remaining two of the seven were
Shrew, not consistent in the speech-headings of the Induction
(as Greg notices) and irregular in form, but with consistent
speech-headings in the text, along with *Ado,* not characterized.

Thus the plays of the first class have three of the four
texts with notably consistent speech-headings, and none with
notably inconsistent, while the second class has all the notably
inconsistent, and only one of the consistent, though even it is
not completely so. The division is notable and for the second
class approaches consistency. It is also evident that Shakspere
himself did not normally edit his speech-headings to consistency.
This would not mean, however, that he may not have had help
from others in acquiring a greater degree of either consistency
or inconsistency. But the almost complete correlation between
plays of the second class and notably inconsistent speech-headings must mean that Shakspere himself could be notably inconsistent in this matter, and that in this group he had no help
toward regularity from copyists.

It is apparent that in the comedies, regularity of speech-
headings has a suspicious coincidence with copying, appearing
in two out of three of the fully regular cases. Further, it occurs almost wholly in the comedies. For while Dr. McKerrow
includes *King John* of the histories and *Macbeth* of the tragedies, Sir Walter Greg comments "*King John* is at best a
doubtful case."[13] None of these plays with regularized speech-
headings has a preceding quarto. The most likely explanation
for excessive regularity of speech-headings in the First Folio is

12 Greg, *First Folio,* p. 113 n.   14 McKerrow, "Shakespeare's Manu-
13 Greg, *First Folio,* p. 113 n.

sophistication in copying. It would seem that Dr. McKerrow has the correct solution. "What, then, is the meaning of this difference between regularity and irregularity in which the speakers' names are shown? Simply, I think, that a play in which the names are irregular was printed from the author's original MS., and that one in which they are regular and uniform is more likely to have been printed from some sort of fair copy, perhaps made by a professional scribe."[14]

Excessive irregularity, on the other hand, shows a heavy incidence upon the early plays, *Labour's Lost* (Q & F), *Well* (first form as *Labour's Won?*), *Errors, Romeo* (Q2 & F),[15] *Titus* (Q & F), *Dream* (Q & F), *Merchant* (Q & F). As I date, all these are before 1595, except *Merchant,* where Sir Walter Greg says "the feature is less marked." Professor J. Dover Wilson, however, would date the original play 1594, so would find no difficulty here. I believe he is certainly correct in positing a revision, which, I think, can be pretty definitely dated. He may, therefore, be correct as to the original date. Revision may account for the division between McKerrow and Greg. Of the other plays which I would place before 1595, *Gentlemen* does not show the characteristic; but we have just seen cause to suspect that this play was sophisticated at copying for the First Folio. This leaves only the history plays, where divided authorship enters into the question for the three parts of *Henry VI,* and where there are numerous unsolved problems in connection with *Richard III.*

Excessive irregularity of speech-headings is thus clearly one characteristic of Shakspere's early work. Evidently the early revisers and copyists were not martinets for regularity. At the reorganization and enlargement in the latter part of 1594, when Shakspere himself became a member and received special duties in the fiscal department, there were doubtless

scripts," *RES,* XI (1935), p. 464.   15 On Q1 of *Romeo,* see *Ibid.,* p. 462, n 1.

changes also in the editorial division, which would have some kind of reflection in the preparation of manuscripts for the stage. But it is possible that routine familiarity on the part of Shakspere also improved the regularity of later work in this respect, but, if so, never hardened into an absolute system. It is likely that a close examination of these early plays would reveal other such stigmata of early work.

Dr. McKerrow was beginning to use in other ways this same principle that inconsistency is likely to indicate the author, and following in his steps, as well as taking strides of his own, Sir Walter Greg has now developed the principle further into his hypothesis of Shakspere's "foul papers,"[16] which we shall have occasion to examine later.

---

16 Greg, *First Folio.* pp. 96ff.

Chapter Seven

HISTORIES AND TRAGEDIES

IN THE FIRST FOLIO

WE MAY NOW check rapidly the histories and tragedies to the categories we have established in connection with the comedies. The histories are arranged, of course, in chronological sequence. All the histories except three are of the first class, divided into acts and scenes, though some are not pleased with the execution of *King John,* while *1 Henry VI* marks the scenes in the third and irregularly in the fifth acts only. Of these seven plays, four have in their background "good" quartos, which are, of course, undivided. *Richard II* was "Printed from [Q of 1615] with some omissions and considerable alterations and corrections from another source."[1] *1 Henry IV* was "Printed from [Q of 1613]."[2] For *2 Henry IV,* "It is uncertain whether this edition was printed from a corrected copy of [Q of 1600, variant issue] or from manuscript. The text shows considerable additions, some omissions, and many variants."[3] For *Richard III,* "The text of this edition differs from that previously published, containing substantial additions and many alterations from another source, but how far it was actually printed from manuscript is uncertain."[4] So in the case of *2 Henry IV,* the variation between quarto and Folio is so great

---

1 Greg, *Bibliography,* I, 228.
2 Greg, *Bibliography,* I, 240.
3 Greg, *Bibliography,* I, 273. Sir Walter has omitted to mention the scenes of

2 Henry IV in the First Folio—a most comforting lapse to ordinary mortals.
4 Greg, *Bibliography,* I, 232.

as to make it uncertain whether the quarto was used. In the case of *Richard III* the differences are also substantial, with relative role of manuscript and quarto in dispute; in *Richard II*, there are considerable alterations and corrections. Only in *1 Henry IV* is the variation not notable.

The reason for this variation is readily apparent. For the comedies, the quartos were checked to manuscripts of their own class, the second, if not to their ultimate originals. So there was no great variation. But for the histories the manuscripts chosen for reproduction were of the first class, which was likely to involve considerable variation, at least in details, from the quarto versions. Consequently, there is considerable variation in the histories, in one case enough to cause doubt as to whether the quarto has been used at all, in another nearly as much. In only one of the four instances is the variation not notable, why does not appear from our present order of facts.[5]

Of the three histories which do not belong to the first class, two, *2* and *3 Henry VI*, are from the original undivided stage manuscripts, with minor actors named in them.[6] Presumably there were no available manuscripts here of either the first or the second class, and certainly the "bad" quartos would not have been practicable for copies. So the old stage copy was used in each case, either the actual copy, or a copy of it. More likely the actual copy, since actors are still named and since there is no indication of fresh copying, and if there had been copying, it would likely at this date have been from a divided copy of some kind, though if the plays had not been revived since the custom changed, then all the stage copies would presumably still be of the old undivided type. In any case, it would seem indicated that there was no copy of the first class available for checking. Since manuscripts of the first class are in the direct succession from the author's manuscript, this is a

5 See above, p. 95.   6 See above, p. 40.

significant fact for these plays, where both original authorship
and ownership are in dispute.

The third history not of the first class is *Henry V*, which,
as it stands in the First Folio, is of the second class, with acts
only. "Five acts in verse and prose, with entries of Chorus in
verse at the beginning, in the middle of Act I, at the beginning of Acts II and III, and at the beginning and end of
Act V; the first headed 'Enter Prologue' and the last serving
as epilogue."[7] Modern versions are divided by the four choruses. Thus the first act of the First Folio is divided into the
first and second acts, the second act becomes the third, while
the third is made up of the third and the fourth of the First
Folio, the fifth act remaining the fifth. If this is the correct
solution, as it appears certainly to be, then these act-headings
were inserted into an undivided manuscript, where the divisions
were indicated only by the choruses. The inserter missed the
first chorus, thus throwing his numbering off, and remedied
matters when he came to his last internal chorus, which had
to mark the fifth act, by blundering a division for Act IV into
the midst of the battle scenes. Such blundering can hardly be
charged to any stage official. It would seem, then, that the basic
manuscript for *Henry V* was undivided save for the choruses,
and that someone blunderingly attempted to mark the acts with
relation to them.

It seems likely, therefore, that here, as in the case of *2*
and *3 Henry VI*, no manuscript of the first class was available
for checking, so that, for the three, undivided stage copy was
used. The parallel extends even to the fact that there was a
"bad" quarto for *Henry V*, which, of course, would not have
served for copy. There is also considerable evidence, none of it
conclusive, I think, for an earlier form of *Henry V*, preceding
the three parts of *Henry VI*, though the "bad" quarto does

7 Greg, *Bibliography*, I, 269.

not represent it, at least not fully. At any rate, the history of *Henry V* is irregular, and the form of its printing in the First Folio in some way reflects that irregularity.

When we look for extras, *2 Henry IV* has a special, apologetic epilogue at court for its Oldcastle misdemeanor, and a table of *dramatis personae*. *Henry VIII* has a prologue and an epilogue, but there are no further graces for the histories than these and those we have already noticed.

Our examination makes it clear that six out of the ten histories were checked to manuscripts of the first class, and that at the expense of considerable trouble in transcription. A seventh was partially from manuscript of the first class, the remainder of it being from manuscript of the second class. Three were from undivided stage copy, two of them showing the names of actors. Presumably the effort was in all cases to present manuscripts of the first class, so that the partial failure in one case and the complete failure in three likely means that no manuscripts of the first class were available for these, and so stage copies of them were used, perhaps actual stage copies as indicated by the jottings for actors in *2* and *3 Henry VI*, since we would expect these to have been omitted if special copies had been made.

When we turn to the tragedies, the arrangement is significant. All seven tragedies of the second class (with acts only or undivided) come first, except one, followed by all five tragedies of the first class (with acts and scenes) except one; and, as we have seen,[8] that one, *Cymbeline,* was attached to the end of the tragedies because of the difficulty of classifying it. For the plays of the second class, the original plan was that the undivided *Troilus* should follow the undivided *Romeo,* but *Troilus* was pulled, eventually being placed at the beginning of the tragedies, and *Timon* took its place. Thus three of the four undivided plays (*Romeo, Troilus, Timon*) were in

8 See above, pp. 52–53.

effect grouped together originally, the fourth, *Antony*, being added at the original end of the tragedies, this fact raising the question of why it should have received special treatment. Of the three tragedies divided into acts only, *Coriolanus* and *Titus* were originally placed first, before the three undivided, and *Caesar* was placed after them. Further, according to this original plan three plays of the second class prepared on good quartos should have come together (*Titus, Romeo, Troilus*). These six tragedies of the second class were followed by four of the first class, divided into both acts and scenes (*Macbeth, Hamlet* partially, *Lear, Othello*). Here again the latter three have "good" quarto forbears and are placed physically together. So in both the comedies and the tragedies plays with "good" quartos are grouped in the First Folio. In the histories, chronology had taken precedence in the arrangement.

There was thus an evident sorting of the tragedies according to the type of manuscript, whether of the first or of the second class, and within these types according to kind of copy. Those who made the original arrangement of the tragedies placed the tragedies of the second class (acts only or undivided) first, followed by the tragedies of the first class (acts and scenes). Within the second class, they distinguished almost completely between those with acts and those which were undivided. Finally, they placed an undivided play of the second class at the original end, and later added the doubtful tragedy *Cymbeline* of the first class to make the final end. They were certainly aware that they were dealing with different types of manuscript, by whatever names they called the types.

Some of these tragedies had good precedent quartos, and here, for those of the first class, the history of the histories repeats itself. For *Lear,* "The text printed in [F] . . . differs extensively from that previously published both in persistent variations of reading and through considerable additions and more considerable omissions. That it is largely derived from an independent source is certain, but opinion differs as to whether it was actually printed from manuscript or from a much corrected copy of [the true Q of 1608]."[9] *Othello* had not been printed till 1622, when, alone of the quartos before the First Folio, it was divided into "Five acts (the third not marked) in verse and prose."[10] In 1623, the play was divided into "Five acts and scenes in verse and prose," and "The text here printed is fuller than that previously published, from whose readings it also frequently differs, and was evidently derived from a different source."[11]

For both plays, the text varies so widely as to make it doubtful if the preceding quarto had been used, and in both cases, the manuscript standard is of the first class, whereas the *Lear* quarto had been of the undivided early form, which form had come before the time of the First Folio to have the acts marked, but not the scenes, as in *Othello*. So manuscripts of the first class have been substituted for stage copies of the second class, whether or not they were checked on the preceding quartos.

Hamlet, of course, presents a grand hash, with "bad" quarto undivided, "good" quarto undivided, and Folio divided into acts and scenes as in the first class through II, 2. There could hardly be a greater scramble to unscramble. Canny Sir Walter Greg goes only so far for the Folio as "Printed from manuscript, and differing from the text of [the preceding "good" quartos] both in respect of additions and omissions."[12] We had better emulate his well-tried discretion, and notice simply that even if a quarto should have been used, still the manuscript selected as standard for checking was of the first class as far as II, 2. We should remember, however, that copies of the author's manuscript sometimes carried over the full di-

9 Greg, *Bibliography*, I, 400.
10 Greg, *Bibliography*, II, 523.
11 Greg, *Bibliography*, II, 523.

12 Greg, *Bibliography*, I, 312.
13 Greg, *Bibliography*, I, 197.

vision into acts and scenes. It would thus appear that if in any of our three out of five cases, a quarto, which would have been undivided (except for *Othello*), was used, there was such change in checking to the first class as to swamp the quarto. Whatever was done, it is clear that for these plays there was considerable variation between the manuscripts of the first class and those of the second, including the undivided stage copies. This we found to be the case also in the histories.

When we turn to tragedies of the second class, three of the seven (*Coriolanus, Titus, Caesar*) are divided into acts only. Of these, *Titus* had a previous quarto, where history, as shown in the comedies, repeats itself. "The second scene (not marked) of the third act appeared for the first time in this edition . . . otherwise the text is a reprint of [the Q of 1611]."[13] Here the quarto has been checked by a manuscript of its own class, which at this period would be divided into acts only.[14] Consequently, there is little change. If a manuscript of the first class was available, it was not used.

The remaining four tragedies (*Romeo*, the vagrant and suspect *Troilus*, the suspect *Timon*, and *Antony*) are undivided. The case of *Romeo and Juliet* is analogous to that of *Henry V* in that it was evidently divided originally by sonnet choruses. In the "bad" quarto of 1597 the first of these is labeled as "The Prologue"; in the "good" quarto of 1599, this sonnet "Prologue" is by "Corus," and there is another sonnet "Chorus" to divide Acts I and II. Evidently we have lost the other three sonnet dividers and the sonnet epilogue, all of which would have been by Chorus. The reprint of 1609 reproduces 1599, but the First Folio omits the prologue-sonnet-chorus. In general, however, the verdict is that the First Folio was "printed from [the Quarto of 1609.]"[15] Here there was apparently no checking to manuscript of any kind, not even for

14 There had been apparently at least occasion for such an up-to-date man- uscript. See below, p. 104.
15 Greg, *Bibliography*, I, 235.

act-divisions. It is probably significant that the "good" quarto of *Romeo and Juliet* was singled out by McKerrow along with *Errors* as outstandingly irregular in its speech-headings, which we have seen to be characteristic of Shakspere's early work. The most authentic copy had probably been used in 1598. At any rate, in 1623 there was no attempt particularly to improve it.

For *Troilus* in the First Folio, "The text printed in this and subsequent editions contains some lines not in that previously published, and clearly made use of an independent source, but whether it was actually printed from manuscript or from a corrected copy of [the Quarto of 1609] is uncertain."[16] Since the publishers of 1609 boast that they had their text without the consent of the company, that manuscript would not be available in 1621–23. The company did, however, evidently have an old undivided manuscript,[17] which as evidently had not been brought up to date by the insertion of act-divisions, and the company did not now insert them. Since their stated aim and their proved practice was to use the complete originals, they apparently had no manuscript of the first class for *Troilus*, another significant fact for authorship.

It is not suprising that the suspect *Timon* should be undivided, especially in view of its condition. But the case of *Antony* is puzzling, since it is a late play and there is nothing else to suggest irregularity.

We are now in position to check our findings against the characteristics of surviving "Prompt-Books," where division into acts and scenes is generally indicative of authors' autographs; division into acts, of nonautograph copies; lack of division, of early nonautograph stage copies. First, for plays having "good" quartos, the probability would be by analogy that the four "good" quartos of the histories were checked to the author's autograph, three of the "good" quartos of

16 Greg, *Bibliography*, I, 414.
17 Miss Alice Walker (*M.L.R.*, XLV,

459–64) believes that at least two manuscripts were available to those

the tragedies to the author's autograph, one to nonautograph copy, two to undivided copies. The "good" quartos themselves had been undivided. Thus in the tragedies two of the "good" quartos remain without division, but three are checked to the first class, only one to the divided second class. For histories and tragedies combined, the score is seven checked to the first class, one to the second, two remaining undivided. Thus for the histories and tragedies, editorial preference was clearly for the first class, which by analogy should have been or should closely have represented Shakspere's autograph.

In the three cases of variance (*Romeo, Troilus, Titus*) out of ten, there must have been some counterbalancing difficulty. *Troilus* and *Titus* are plays of disputed authorship, and the publishers of the quarto of *Troilus* had boasted that the company had not been able to prevent publication of this play, "neuer stal'd with the Stage, neuer clapper-clawd with the palmes of the vulger." *Romeo* had a "bad" quarto which was replaced by a "good" one. There is some form of irregularity behind all three of these plays.

The same tendency is apparent in the plays with "bad" quartos. For the histories, *2*, and *3 Henry VI* are undivided, and all know the disputes which rage around them and their "bad" quartos. *Henry V* was in fact also undivided, and had a "bad" quarto. After II, 2, *Hamlet* is undivided, and we have already mentioned *Romeo and Juliet*, both plays with "bad" quartos. So histories and tragedies with "bad" quartos mostly remain undivided stage copies, though *Henry V* has acts bungled in, and *Hamlet* has acts and scenes through II, 2 only.

For undivided plays without quartos, "good" or "bad," *Timon* is of disputed authorship and took the physical position of *Troilus* when that play was at first removed from the First Folio. Only *Antony* of the undivided plays does not have a

who prepared *Troilus* for the First   348–49.
Folio. See Hillebrand, ed. *Troilus,* pp.

chequered and suspect history. Lack of division is thus coupled with lack of regularity in all cases except *Antony*, the irregularity usually involving some point of authorship, either divided authorship, and/or revision of an older play.[18] The implication is that for these undivided plays as a class, though there might be individual exceptions, Shakspere had not produced a full-dress authorial manuscript of the first class, in acts and scenes, else at least those with "good" quartos would have been checked to these. If so, then so far as Shakspere was concerned, these undivided stage manuscripts were the most authentic that had ever existed, and Heminges and Cundall were fully justified in considering them to be the best available.

In contrast to the undivided plays, there is no urgent suspicion of *Caesar* and *Coriolanus,* of the second class divided into acts, as there was none of the undivided *Antony*. Why divided manuscripts of the first class were not available for *Caesar*, *Antony*, and *Coriolanus* is not directly apparent, unless no such ready-made copies were available, while good stage copies were. Another grouping suggests that at least good stage copies were available for *Caesar* and *Coriolanus*. Six out of our ten plays of the second class among the histories and the tragedies (*2*, and *3 Henry VI, Romeo, Troilus, Timon, Antony*) are undivided. *Henry V* really belongs to undivided plays, since its act-divisions were evidently bungled in according to the choruses by someone inexpert in such matters. This leaves really only three plays of the second class divided into acts, *Coriolanus*, *Titus*, and *Caesar*. "Titus, and Vespatian" is in a list of plays *c.*1619–20 probably suggested for performance at Court.[19] It would presumably have had some freshening up of its form to the standards of those days, which in the case of *Woodstock* and *Ironsides* included notation of the act-divisions in the left margin. *Caesar* shows sufficient signs of regularization to cause

18 This fact, in turn, would occasion incompletely controlled ownership, so that the company could not prevent "stolne and surreptitious" copies from

Sir Walter Greg to class it with "official" "Prompt-Books," though it is divided only into acts, while his "official" six are fully regularized into acts and scenes. The act-divisions likely came into the left margins with such regularization as it received, and probably indicate that *Caesar* also had been recently in production. For *Coriolanus*, I know of no convincing clue, though Sir Walter thinks, "Since *Coriolanus* was originally intended to open the section of Tragedies, this may well have been introduced at the time of printing."[20] If that had been the motive, one would have expected full dress of acts and scenes, not acts merely. The probability, not certainty, is that *Coriolanus*, *Titus*, and *Caesar* had recently been in production, so that availability may have been a weighty reason for using stage copies for them. But we still have no indication as to why undivided stage copy was used for *Antony*.

We do, however, have the fundamental fact that in the histories and tragedies manuscripts of the first-class were preferred, and that the eventual exemplar more or less faithfully reproduced was likely Shakspere's autograph. Undivided stage-copies were second choice, though this may have been the only kind of copy that had ever existed for these. At least, those responsible did make some effort to take the author's own "unblotted" originals as the standard.

---

getting into print.   346.
19 Chambers, *William Shakespeare*, II,   20 Greg, *First Folio*, p. 407

Chapter Eight

THE HEART OF THE MATTER

AS WE LOOK back, certain facts are clear-cut. When a play of the second class (in acts only) has a "good" quarto, as in *Ado, Labour's, Dream, Merchant, Titus,* the text in the First Folio and quarto shows little variance, and the verdict of modern opinion is that the quarto has each time been used to prepare the copy for the First Folio. The reason for this relationship is clear. As we have seen from our examination of plots, surviving early manuscripts, and early quartos, the stage copies for men's companies in the early period were usually undivided, since most plays did not have any extraneous matter to be inserted at the act-divisions. Two of our early undivided manuscripts, *Woodstock* and *Ironsides,* have apparently had acts indicated at later revival, when notation of acts in the left margin had become the custom. It would appear that the same kind of thing has happened to some of the originally undivided Shaksperean stage copies, whether the original stage copy was still existent or only a copy of it survived. The stage copies themselves would seem to have remained much the same, having received only such trivial external interference as we find in *Woodstock* and *Ironsides,* which went through a similar process. Unless there was more than one copy of the stage copy, it follows that the original stage copy was not lost by publication of a good quarto. Conversely, the printers of the good quartos, had a good copy of the stage copy, whether the original copy or a copy of it. To this extent their copy was authentic, whether stolen and surreptitious or not. If they stole— most emphatically, I do not say they did—they had the sense to steal authentic stage copy. The only question would be why, while they were about it, they didn't steal the author's original. They had stage copy, and for plays generally they advertized consistently "as acted;" presumably they thought that more appealing.

The evidence is equally clear for plays of the first class, with acts and scenes in the First Folio, when they have precedent good quartos. Seven of the ten histories are of the first class, and four of these have good quartos. Some of the corresponding four folio texts are so widely divergent as to leave doubt whether the quarto has been used at all. In only one case, *1 Henry IV*, is there no statement that the variation is considerable. For the tragedies of the first class, *Lear* differs extensively from the quarto version, *Othello* apparently did not use its contemporary quarto at all (second class), and *Hamlet*, divided through II. 2. was from manuscript, diverging from the quartos. From both the histories and the tragedies, it is apparent and clear-cut, that manuscripts of the first class almost always differed materially from the stage copies which had been used for the quartos. Also, the ideal for the histories and tragedies was to avoid manuscripts of the second class, of which only three were used, one of these having been preceded by a "good" quarto, which narrowly conforms to it, as is the rule for the second class. Against four and a piece of the first class, and three of the second class, there are four wholly undivided copies among the tragedies, two of which had previous quartos, one of which used the previous quarto with little variation, while one, *Troilus,* necessarily was checked to a different manuscript, even if it used the quarto at all, as perhaps it did, though it varies from it considerably.

It must, however, be a significant fact that for the histories and tragedies the "good" quartos were checked usually to manuscripts of the first class, though that meant a great deal more work than if they had been checked to manuscripts of the second class, as in the comedies, where exactly the opposite policy prevailed. It does not seem likely that such a clearcut and diametrically opposite policy for the comedies as against the histories and tragedies could have been the result of mere availability of material. For the "good" quartos, the editorial policy in the comedies was to check to standards of their own class as these standards had come to exist by 1621. For the histories, the policy was as uniform to check to the standards of the first class. For the tragedies, the policy was predominantly to check to the first class or, failing that, to the old undivided type of the second class, without adding act-divisions as had become customary by 1621. There is evidently much less of editorial sophistication in the histories and tragedies.

It would appear, then, that where a "good" quarto was checked to a manuscript of the second class there is small variation in the Folio text. This agreement was due to collusion, and the collusion was upon stage copy at that. The quarto was itself from undivided stage copy, and was checked to undivided stage copy but with acts marked in the margin as in the later period. Both go back ultimately, therefore, to the same copy and should enable us to reproduce the stage copy. There is still the question of how well the stage copy represented Shakspere's autograph. And we shall still have to face the vicissitudes through which the stage copy may itself have passed, before quarto, and between quarto and Folio. On Shakspere's autograph, the plays of the second class throw no light directly.

But where a good quarto was checked to a manuscript of the first class, we have at least one manuscript by which to criticize another. The one used for the First Folio should have been more directly from Shakspere's autograph, even if that autograph had been used as a "Prompt-Book." But again a great deal depends upon how faithfully the autograph was copied, how many times, on what principles it was checked, etc.

It becomes apparent also that for the histories and trage-dies, reached about the end of 1622 a different set of standards became operative. Now the ideal was to print from the first class; that is, the nearest thing to the author's autograph. Con-sequently, if "good" quartos are used at all, they are checked, with exception of *Romeo*, *Troilus*, and *Titus* among the tragedies, to manuscripts of the first class. Only if manuscripts of the first class are not available do those responsible use those of the second class, either the old type of stage copies undi-vided, as in *2* and *3 Henry VI*, *Romeo*, *Troilus*, *Timon*, *An-tony*, or the newer type, divided into acts, as bunglingly in *Henry V*, which really belongs to the undivided, and in *Corio-lanus*, *Titus*, *Caesar*. They evidently preferred manuscripts of the first class. Failing these, they used the old stage copies, only four of which had inserted divisions to become technically of the second class.

In this the editors were right, of course, since the author's original manuscript was of the first class, and the original stage copies from these were undivided. We are thus likely in the Folio to be generally much nearer to Shakspere's own manu-script in the histories and tragedies than we are in the comedies. For in the comedies five of the seven plays of the first class are copies, in various known ways sophisticated. Nor should we place too much dependence upon the other two, without thorough proving. The seven of the second class are from stage copies, not from originals. These seven stage copies of the second class, however, are probably less sophisticated than at

---

1 "Of the thirty-six plays in the First Folio fourteen had previously ap-peared in what are generally reputed 'good' quartos, and for the majority of these a quarto was used, with more or less correction, as copy for the folio" (Greg, *Folio*, p. 159). "In eleven cases certainly: over *2 Hen-ry IV* and *Othello* opinion is still di-

least five of the seven plays of the first class, for the former were merely stage copies, probably untampered, while the five copies of the first class were "literary," where we must fear a great deal more of conscious "improvement."

But for all three divisions, comedies, histories, tragedies, it was the ideal to use manuscript as the standard, so that, unless *Romeo* be the exception, in no case was a quarto simply reprinted without some addition; in some cases it is doubtful if a preceding quarto was used at all;[1] in every case of use, the quarto was primarily an agent for transmitting manuscript to print. On this point Heminges and Cundall unquestionably have won their case. They did use manuscripts as their standards, not quartos.

But a great deal depends upon the kind of manuscripts they used. What actually do they say? Only that the "stolne, and surreptitious copies . . . are now offer'd to your view cur'd, and perfect of their limbes; and all the rest, absolute in their numbers, as he conceiued thẽ . . . wee haue scarse receiued from him a blot in his papers." They do not say or imply that they printed from Shakspere's unblotted papers. They say only that they had received unblotted originals of these plays, and that now these plays are printed complete as they had them. They emphasize the genuine completeness, not the fidelity to minute detail.

They did use manuscript as their standard, not the quartos. What kind of manuscript? It is clear that they would not and did not cast the originals before the compositors. The problem was in each case to procure an authentic copy. Their use of the quartos has shown us what kind of copy. For the histories and the tragedies, their aim in all cases had been, a copy of the first

---

vided; *Hamlet* is generally believed to have been printed from a manuscript, but even this has recently been questioned. It would make a neater pattern if in all cases quartos had been used" (Greg, *Folio*, p. 159 n). For a fuller statement, see Greg, *Folio*, pp. 428–29.

class, which in form at least, is nearest the author's autograph; but failing this they used the stage copy, still undivided, or with acts inserted after the new guise. In the majority of cases here, the undivided quartos were replaced by or checked to manuscripts of the first class, which would be or would represent the author's original in form and presumably in content. Why in other cases they used the stage copies, undivided or with acts only, instead of the author's originals is not directly apparent. But they would justly regard these as next best. Unfortunately, they had not formulated this procedure when the comedies were prepared in 1621. There even the plays of the first class had been sophisticated in copying, and quartos had not been checked to the first class but to copies of the second class, the type from which they had originally been made. With these facts before us we are now better prepared to understand the statements attributed to Heminges and Cundall.

Chapter Nine

LITERARY GENETICS OF THE PHRASE

"MAIMED AND DEFORMED"

JOHN HEMINGES and Henry Cundall did not originate the epithets "maimed and deformed" as applied to plays.
In his prefatory letter "To the Reader" for *Philaster. Or,
Loue lies a Bleeding,* "The second Impression, corrected, and
amended," (1622) Thomas Walkley had developed a figure out
of the title and the circumstances of that play up to these
epithets. "Courteous Reader. *Philaster,* and *Arethusa* his loue,
haue laine so long a bleeding, by reason of some dangerous and
gaping wounds, which they receiued in the first Impression, that
it is wondered how they could goe abroad so long, or trauaile
so farre as they haue done. Although they were hurt neither
by me, nor the Printer; yet I knowing and finding by experience,
how many well-wishers they haue abroad, haue aduentured to
bind vp their wounds, & to enable them to visite vpon better
tearmes, such friends of theirs, as were pleased to take knowledge of them, so mained [*sic*] and deformed, as they at the first
were; and if they were then gracious in your sight, assuredly
they will now finde double fauour, being reformed, and set forth
suteable, to their birth, and breeding."[1]

While Walkley admits that the first edition of *Philaster*
was "maimed and deformed" as to text, yet it was completely
regular in its entry to print. On January 10, 1620, Walkley

1 Greg, *Bibliography,* III, 1217.

"Entred for his copie vnder the hande of Mr Tauernor and Mr Iaggard warden A Play Called Philaster."[2] By the entry, sanctioned by a warden, Walkley claimed this copy against all other members of the stationers' guild, and there is no indication that his right to the copy was challenged. He also had the hand of "Mr Tauernor" for the acceptability of its content.

It happens to be important to notice who Master John Taverner[3] was. On March 22, 1620, William Jaggard "Entered for his copie vnder the handes of Master TAUERNOR and Master *Swinhowe* warden. A booke Called *The Decameron* of Master JOHN BOCCACE, Florentine." A side note states, "recalled by my lord of CANTERBURYES command," and Arber comments, "So this edition of BOCCACIO was licensed by the Bishop of LONDON through his secretary, and that license afterwards revoked by the Primate."[4] As far as I have observed, Taverner makes his first appearance in S.R. December 4, 1612 and following, as licenser of pamphlets connected with the death of Prince Henry.[5] He goes out significantly. On May 14, 1621, *Wither's Motto* was entered under the hands of Master Lownes warden, "PROUIDED, that it be not printed vntill he bring further aucthority."[6] The book was entered the following June 16, to be printed "as it is corrected by Master TAUERNOR."[7]

The official record for John Taverner runs, "Matric. pens. from TRINITY, c. 1597. 2nd s. of Peter, of Hexton, Herts., and grandson of Richard, clerk of the Signet to Henry VIII, and of Woodeaton, Oxon. School, Westminster. Scholar, 1599; B.A. 1601–2; M.A. 1605. Incorp. at Oxford, 1606. Secretary to Dr. King, Bishop of London. Professor of Music at Gresham College, 1610–38. Ord. deacon (London) Dec. 24, 1620; priest, Mar. 13, 1624–5. V. of Tillingham, Essex, 1624–9. V.

2 Greg, *Bibliography*, I, 31.
3 *A Transcript of the Stationers' Registers*, ed. Edward Arber, III, 534, p. 244.
4 *Transcript*, ed. Arber, III, 667, p. 311.
5 *Transcript*, ed. Arber, III, 505ff., p. 230.
6 *Transcript*, ed. Arber, IV, 53, p. 15.
7 *Transcript*, ed. Arber, IV, 56, p. 18.

of Hexton, Herts., 1629–38. R. of Stoke Newington, Middlesex, 1629–38. Died Aug. 1638. Buried at Stoke Newington. M.I. Will dated, Aug. 26; proved, Aug. 29, 1638 (*Vis. of Herts.,* 1634; *Al. Oxon.; D.N.B.; Clutterbuck,* III, 10)."[8] Surely not even modern agnosticism can suspect any "monkey-business" in the license dealings of this august personage.

Taverner was thus certainly one of the regular licensers for the Bishop of London. Naturally his tour of duty as licenser coincided closely with the tenure of Dr. King as Bishop. But throughout this period only Taverner of the licensers is given as authority for the license of plays in every instance when Sir George Buck is not, and in the first instance of Taverner as play licenser, May 23, 1614, both he and Buck are given as authority for the license; entered "vnder the hand*es* of Mr Taverno^r Sr George Bucke and m^r ffeild warden a play booke called Hogge hath lost his pearle."[9] Sir Walter Greg comments, "The double license is unusual and perhaps an error. Tavernor may, like Segar, have been Buc's deputy."[10] More likely the double entry was in this first instance due to bepuzzlement as to how Taverner's licenses were to be recorded. Thereafter Taverner is cited alone, without Buck. Taverner was evidently an authorized substitute for Buck, but he was not Buck's deputy, as Segar had been under the previous bishop.

With the establishment of this fact, a theory falls which was confidently announced by Crompton Rhodes,[11] very hesitantly accepted by Sir Edmund Chambers,[12] and taken for a time on faith by Sir Walter Greg, who later recanted. "My belief is that at any rate in the first quarter of the seventeenth century the Wardens of the Company took the responsibility for allowing the entrance of any play which had been licensed for

8 John and J. A. Venn, *Alumni Cantabrigienses.*
9 Greg, *Bibliography,* I, 28.
10 Greg, *Bibliography,* I, 462.
11 R. C. Rhodes, *Shakespeare's First Folio,* pp. 27, 31.
12 Chambers, *William Shakespeare,* I, 100, 129.

acting by the Master of the Revels."[13] Obviously, Taverner cannot be fitted into any such theory. He certainly licensed for print, and exactly the same form of entry was used for Buck and for his deputy Segar from 1607, as it was also for other types of material. Besides it is known from independent sources that Buck did license plays for print, and Herbert later alleged that Buck had regularly so licensed plays, as Sir Walter had noted. On other grounds, Sir Walter later decided that the theory "should be rejected."[14]

Further, as early as June 1, 1599, Canterbury and London in the persons of Whitgift and Bancroft are recorded in S.R. as having ordered among other things, "That noe playes be printed excepte they bee allowed by suche as haue aucthorytie."[15] Gradually thereafter the custom grew to cite the Bishop's licenser (any one of them could act) in the entry till Buck became the licenser in 1607. Buck is first cited S.R. in connection with the *Fleer*. On May 13, 1606,[16] John Trundell and John Busby had a provisional entry "for their Copie by warrant from Mr Norton vnder his hand." As warden, Norton had certified that he was satisfied of the ownership. But it was "provided that they are not to printe yt tell they bringe good aucthoritie and licence for the doinge thereof." Consequently, on November 21, 1606,[17] John Busby and Arthur Johnson entered the play "by assignem^t from John Trundell . . . formerlie entred to the said John Trundell." The provisional entry was to John Trundell and John Busby. In the meantime Trundell had been replaced by Arthur Johnson. This entry is to legalize that "assignment." The original proviso for "good aucthoritie and licence" is satisfied by the appended notation, "This booke is aucthorised by Sr George Bucke Mr Hartwell & the wardens." Hartwell was certainly the Bishop's licenser. Buck would have

13 Greg, *Editorial Problem*, p. 107.   [f]–[g].
14 Greg, *Editorial Problem*, 2nd ed.,   15 *Transcript*, ed. Arber, III. 677, p. 316.

licensed the play for the stage, and there is no other evidence that he licensed for printing under Bishop Vaughan.

At any rate, Sir George Buck became the regular licenser of plays for print by April 10, 1607. Richard Vaughan had died March 30, 1607, and Thomas Ravis succeeded officially June 2, 1607. So Buck began in the inter-regnum, as it were, a fact which probably means that the adjustment was made from above, on the suggestion, or the insistence, of the Office of the Revels (Tilney and Buck). Under Bishop Ravis, Tilney (titular), Buck (actual), and Buck's deputy Segar all acted. Buck acted regularly, Segar acted October 4, 1608, and from January 26 through March 10, 1609. Tilney acted only once, June 29, 1607. Wilson, a Bishop's licenser, also acted once, May 2, 1608. In effect, therefore, the Master of the Revels took over the licensing of plays for print after the death of Bishop Vaughan. I know nothing to indicate exactly how this arrangement was stated officially.

When Tilney had died and Buck had succeeded officially, Taverner, as licenser for Bishop King, was Buck's only substitute. In a way, Buck became a special licenser of plays for the Bishop, with special jurisdiction over plays. It was thus natural for Taverner of the Bishop's staff to be designated as Buck's substitute. At any rate, it is surely now certain that Buck licensed plays for print as well as for the stage. With 1614, Taverner of the Bishop's licensers began to supplement Buck in this function. Thus Taverner's license for the printing of *Philaster* was completely regular.

The record certifies directly only that Taverner had licensed the play, which means that it was of fit content to be printed, while William Jaggard (who had printed Pavier's wretched quartos) had approved as warden the entry for the

16 Greg, *Bibliography*, I, 21.   17 Greg, *Bibliography*, I, 22.

Stationers' Company. But in view of the evolution of the license to print, Taverner's license has still other implications. This "evolving system of control stems ultimately from the fuller control established by the Privy Council in 1597, whose relevant officials would be the lord chamberlain and the master of the revels. In the period 1598–1603, the official once referred to specifically for 'authority' for publication of a play is the lord chamberlain. By 1607 the master of the revels had established his right to license plays for print. This right was exercised in connection with all of the Shakespearean plays after 1603; *Lear, Pericles, Antony and Cleopatra, Troilus,* as well as upon the plays of others. This license is thus routine for publication and has no necessary connection with license for acting."[18] Thus by 1598, at least the plays of the Shaksperean company called for special procedure, and by 1607, that procedure for all plays was to have the license of the Master of the Revels or of his substitute before entry S.R. After the order of June 1, 1599, no play should have been entered without the license of one of the Bishop's licensers, but we have no way of knowing how well the order was obeyed.

The Lord Chamberlain had taken a hand by 1598 in seeing that at least his players had a chance to defend their property. The Lord Chamberlain, in a different person, found it necessary to repeat or give similar instructions in 1619. After consideration of a letter from the Lord Chamberlain, the Court of the Stationers' Company ordered May 3, 1619, that no plays of the King's men should be printed without their consent; "vppon a letter from the right honorable the Lord Chamberleyne It is thought fitt & so ordered That no playes that his Maiestyes players do play shalbe printed without consent of somme of them."[19]

On June 10, 1637, Philip, Earl of Pembroke and Mont-

18 Baldwin in H. N. Hillebrand, *Troilus and Cressida* (Furness Variorum), pp. 358–59.

19 Greg, *First Folio,* pp. 15–16, 24. W. A. Jackson, *Records of the Court*

gomery, as Lord Chamberlain recapitulated the earlier order of his brother William, Earl of Pembroke, who had preceded him in office. "Wheras complaint was heertofore presented to my Deare brother & predecessor by his Maiestes servantes the Players, that some of the Company of Printers & Stationers had procured, published & printed diuerse of their bookes of Comædyes, Tragedyes, Cronicle Historyes, and the like, which they had (for the speciall service of his Maiestye & for their owne vse) bought and provided at very Deare & high rates, By meanes wherof not onely they themselues had much preiudice, but the bookes much corruption to the iniury and disgrace of the Authors; And therupon the Masters & Wardens of the company of printers & stationers were advised by my Brother to take notice therof & to take Order for the stay of any further Impression of any of the Playes or Interludes of his Maiestes servantes without their consentes."[20]

In 1598, Shakspere's company was the Lord Chamberlain's men and had invoked the power of their patron. When the company became the King's men in 1603, they were still under the Lord Chamberlain, who would still presumably remain mindful of them. So in the emergency of 1619, and again in 1637, they appealed to have the same prohibition renewed as the original one of about 1598.

How then did the Stationers' Company proceed to see that this original order was obeyed? It was not considered to be a matter to require direct record. A few incidental jottings which happen to survive show that under the early order some plays of Shakspere's company were referred to authority, once specified as the Lord Chamberlain. The instructions of the licensing authorities in 1599 were that all plays should have authority before being entered. This order need mean only that all plays should be licensed for content before entry, and ap-

of the Stationers' Company 1602–1640, p. 110. 20 Greg, *First Folio*, pp. 24–25; Malone Society, *Collections*, II, 384.

parently it was evoked by certain satirical tendencies in plays, and does not necessarily show any concern for ownership. I do not know of any evidence 1597–98, 1619, or 1637 that the Lord Chamberlain in any way communicated his wishes to the licensing authorities. But when in 1607, the Master of the Revels, an official of the Lord Chamberlain, became the licenser of plays for print, surely he would be expected by the Lord Chamberlain to keep his eyes open to the property rights of the King's men. And surely the King's men would take the necessary steps to improve his eyesight now and then, as they are known to have done in various matters.[21]

Apparently, however, not sufficient attention has been paid to exactly what the Lord Chamberlain ordered. He did not order in any known instance that plays which had belonged to these actors should never be printed, but that their plays should not be printed without consent. Nor did he say anything specifically about reprints. In 1619, the consent is specifically that of "his Maiestes servantes." The Stationers in 1619 considered that this prohibition covered all "playes that his Maiestyes players do play." Thus any offered play in which they had played was to be referred to the King's men for consent.

But this would not mean that the King's men could automatically and of mere whim refuse consent. There would still be the question of whether they could prove a sufficient property right to outweigh that of the person proposing to print. There are things called laws. The Lord Chamberlain's order simply assured adjudication so that the King's men could protect their rights. But it could give them no rights they did not already have. Unfortunately, we do not have the facts of adjudication in any case, and can only judge by results. But it must be apparent that if a would-be publisher had copy which he could prove to be legally his, then the fact that any group of actors considered

21 "There can be little doubt that someone in authority had been making inquiries about plays that it was intended to print and had given a

that it once was or still was legally theirs could make no legal difference. Under the conditions of the early nineties, with so many companies acting at various times in as various plays, it must have been very difficult to determine justly who did own a play, even legally, let alone morally. And until we have a better command of the facts in each case it might be more charitable to be less anachronistically righteous in our bestowal of opprobrious terms.

There is no suggestion, of course, that each case of difference became a Star Chamber matter. Most likely there would normally be compromise, for the fault would not inherently be that of the would-be publisher, who presumably would already have been parted from his money, but of the person from whom he had procured the copy, "stolne and surreptitious" and "maimed and deformed" though it might be. The hypothetical rascals would already have injured both parties to this deal. Faced with such a situation, various persons are known even to have supplied a decent copy to replace the deficient one. The settlement between publisher and actors could have been wholly amicable.

At any rate, it is clear that in some cases the actors did not, and even could not, legally prevent legal publication of some play they would have preferred to keep out of print. The publishers of *Troilus and Cressida* in 1609, properly licensed by Buck, say of all Shakspere's plays, "by the grand possessors wills I beleeue you should haue prayd for them rather then beene prayd," and the lack of publication bears them out. They are consequently exultant in being able to publish this play. What happened behind the scenes in the case of *Troilus* we do not know, but the play was published legally, and with the boast that publication was against the will of the "grand possessors."

warning against trespassing upon the   p. 26).
company's preserves" (Greg, *Folio,*

With this background before him, the reader will doubtless already have noticed the significance of the Lord Chamberlain's paraphrase from the petition of the players in his pronounce-ment of May 3, 1619, "not onely they themselues had much preiudice, but the bookes much corruption to the iniury and disgrace of the Authors." Here is the topic statement and the germinal phraseology out of which grew the prefaces of 1623. And these occur *in situ,* as it were. For the Lord Chamberlain was William Herbert, Earl of Pembroke, to whom with his brother Philip, Earl of Montgomery, the First Folio was destined to be dedicated. And it is not to be forgotten that it was Earl Philip as Lord Chamberlain who renewed in 1637 the order of his brother Earl William in 1619. In their dedication "To the most Noble and Incomparable Paire of Brethren," Heminges and Cundall point out that, "since your L.L. haue beene pleas'd to thinke these trifles some-thing, heeretofore; and haue prosequuted both them, and their Authour liuing, with so much fauour: we hope, that (they out-liuing him, and he not hauing the fate, common with some, to be exequutor to his owne writings) you will vse the like indulgence toward them, you haue done vnto their parent. There is a great difference, whether any Booke choose his Patrones, or finde them: This hath done both. For, so much were your L.L. likings of the seuerall parts, when they were acted, as before they were pub-lished, the Volume ask'd to be yours. We haue but collected them, and done an office to the dead, to procure his Orphanes, Guardians; without ambition either of selfe-profit, or fame: onely to keepe the memory of so worthy a Friend, & Fellow aliue, as was our SHAKESPEARE, by humble offer of his playes, to your most noble patronage."

Since Shakspere did not have "the fate, common with some, to be exequutor to his owne writings" (he cannot protect himself against "the iniury and disgrace" of "corruption" in his "bookes"), they have now "collected" them "without ambition of selfe-profit, or fame" (they had complained in 1619 that "they themselues had much preiudice" in profit and fame by the corrupt publication of the plays). Their complaint of 1619 has its echoes here, and the "prosecution" by the Lord Chamberlain which followed had now eventuated in the First Folio, which had "ask'd to be yours" before the plays were published, because of the favor shown "the seuerall parts, when they were acted." This was not idle verbiage. Heminges and Cundall knew and the Herberts knew what lay behind these statements, and we can now trace back dimly to before May 3, 1619. Their nuclear statement of the case in 1619 had so impressed William Herbert, Lord Chamberlain, that he had paraphrased it in his order, and Heminges and Cundall are now in 1623 elaborating on that same theme and in echoing phraseology. If we could see the petition, it would probably show other germinal and germane phraseology, perhaps even indicating already their intention to publish these "bookes of Comædyes, Tragedyes, Cronicle Historyes, and the like," phraseology which adumbrates the title of the First Folio. At least, the title was taking shape in the players' minds for Shakspere's plays as a whole, even though it was already an old, old classification.

The players further expand this fundamental thesis in their address "To the great Variety of Readers," and in doing so connect even more closely with the petition of 1619. "It had bene a thing, we confesse, worthie to haue bene wished, that the Author himselfe had liu'd to haue set forth, and ouerseen his owne writings; But since it hath bin ordain'd otherwise, and he by death departed from that right, we pray you do not envie his Friends, the office of their care, and paine, to haue collected & publish'd them." So far, they are rephrasing the address to the Earls. But now they turn to those of whom they had complained in 1619 that they "had procured, published & printed divers of their bookes" to "the bookes much corruption to the iniury and disgrace of the Authors." In contrast, the players claim in 1623 "so to haue publish'd them, as wherc [*sic*] (before) you were abus'd with diuerse stolne, and surreptitious copies, maimed, and deformed by the frauds and stealthes of iniurious impostors, that expos'd them," you now have the perfect originals. While the "maimed and deformed" of *Philaster* shows through, the fundamental aggravation had occurred before the events which had caused the petition of 1619.

Thanks to brilliant technical work, now known to all as a classic example, the occasion of the petition in 1619 is quite clear. Pavier's collected reprint of his "bad" quartos had revolted the sensibilities of the actors, as well as having reminded them of this long-standing threat to their purses. "All the plays of this collection were printed by William Jaggard, as appears from the devices used, and the initials 'T.P.' that appear on five out of nine title-pages [for six out of ten plays] show the publisher to have been Thomas Pavier."[22] Two of the six, however, are misdated, for whatever reason; two are correctly dated; and two are undated. It should be noticed at once that there was no concealment of either printer or publisher for these six plays. Jaggard proclaims himself the printer by his devices, and for six of the ten plays Pavier proclaims by his initials on the title-pages that he owned the rights to them, as he evidently did. "Pavier had a valid title to the two *Contention* plays, *The Yorkshire Tragedy*, and *1 Sir John Oldcastle*, and a more doubtful one to *Henry V*: no one could claim a title to *Pericles*."[23]

First to examine the allegedly doubtful claim to *Henry V*. On August 4, it would seem certainly in 1600, four books were listed informally as "to be staied," including "Henry the ffift, a booke," the reasons and conditions of the stay not being specified. "Of the four 'staied' plays, *Every Man In His Humour* and *Much Ado About Nothing* were regularly registered later

22 Greg, *Bibliography,* III, 1108.
23 Greg, *Bibliography,* III, 1108.

24 Chambers, *William Shakespeare,* I, 145.

in August 1600 [by different publishers] and published in good texts. There was no Quarto of *As You Like It*. But the stay, whatever its nature, did not prevent the appearance in 1600 of a bad text of *Henry V* or the acknowledgement of copyright when it was transferred on August 14 of that year."[24] The entry on August 14, 1600, runs, "Entred for his Copyes by direction of m[r] white warden vnder his hand wrytinge: These [12] Copyes followinge beinge thing*es* formerlye printed & sett over to the sayd Tho̅ms Pavyer."[25] White as warden certifies that these twelve items had been "formerlye printed," as they had been, under whatever authorization (so that they did not need the authorization of the Bishop's licenser), and "sett over" in the right of these printings to Thomas Pavier. White does not tell us who "sett over" any of these twelve items, but he does certify that *Henry V* among other things, had been "sett over," and his certification was, and must be, accepted of course. Creede had entered *The Famous Victories* May 14, 1594, and had printed an edition in 1598, for whom not stated. He printed also an edition of *Henry V* for Thomas Millington in 1600, and then following the transfer on August 14, 1600, one for Pavier in 1602. If anyone deceived in connection with the two plays it was Creede and not Pavier. It was *Henry V,* not *Famous Victories,* which was "sett over" to Pavier, presumably by Creede, and Creede published an edition for him. The proper authorities certified Pavier's right as valid, and no one is known to have raised an objection to his right.

In the case of *Pericles,* we do not have a transfer to Pavier, but that does not mean that he did not have the right he claimed. On August 4, 1626, the widow of Pavier transferred by official entry S.R. to E. Brewster and R. Birde "Paviers right in Shakesperes plaies or any of them," where Sir Walter Greg notes "This was no doubt intended and was later assumed

25 Greg, *Bibliography*, I, 16.

to include the present piece."[26] Pavier's right was not challenged officially by the Stationers' Company in 1626 or later. There had been entry S.R. of "a booke called. The booke of Pericles Prynce of Tyre" May 20, 1608, to E. Blount, licensed by "Sʳ Geo Buck," which means that it was a play. But no further connection is known for Blount. The present play of *Pericles* was printed for Henry Gosson in two editions under date of 1609. An edition of 1611 was printed by S.S. (Simon Stafford), for whom not stated. It was next "Printed for T.P. 1619." Thus Pavier claimed the right in 1619, and that right was tacitly recognized in 1626, and overtly later. We simply have no official record of the right under which any of these editions of *Pericles* was published. Presumably it was transferred "by note" from one to another. The entry to Blount is the only official entry under which such a chain of legal but not officially recorded transfers could have occurred. Presumably, therefore, his was the original entry.

The upshot is that Pavier claimed the legal rights to six of the ten plays, and we can trace the succession from official records, except in the case of *Pericles,* though Pavier's right to that play also was later officially recognized. No member of the Stationers' Company, therefore, did or presumably could challenge Pavier's rights to these six plays. Pavier could print them individually as often as he liked, and no one could say him nay. Whether there could have been objection to his publication of the six as a collection I do not know. Pavier's brethren had no objections. But anyone who knows these six plays in the form published by Pavier can understand the nauseated revulsion of the actors. They did not consider that *The Yorkshire Tragedy, 1 Sir John Oldcastle,* and *Pericles* even belonged in any pertinent sense to Shakspere, and so these plays are not to be found in the First Folio, though they got attached to the re-issue of the Third Folio in 1664, while *Pericles,* after being in and out

26 Greg, *Bibliography,* I, 420.

of the canon, has managed to stay in for some time now in spite of Heminges and Cundall. Perhaps they feel a bit of revulsion still on that score. The other three plays we know as *Henry V,* and *2* and *3 Henry VI,* but in the fearful mangle of "bad" quartos. The concentrated dose of such an unholy mess naturally revolted the actors—and anyone else who really knew the plays as Shakspere wrote them, as the Herberts are alleged to have known them.

The three plays which are accepted by Heminges and Cundall as Shakspere's were not printed originally under Shakspere's name; it was only toward the very end of the century that his name acquired commercial value, and so was attached to the "bad" quartos of *Merry Wives* and *Hamlet.* His name was not attached to *2* and *3 Henry VI* till 1619 nor to *Henry V* till 1623. Only these three of the mass of "bad" quartos of the nineties were connected with Shakspere's plays. If the manuscripts from which they were printed were in fact "stolne and surreptitious," the big "steal" was not because these three plays of Shakspere's were involved.

Nor had Pavier himself procured or printed originally any one of his three plays which the actors considered to be wretched forms of Shakspere's plays. Pavier had not damaged them. In fact, we grudgingly admit that he had probably made some minor improvements. The beginning of the original offense was as early as 1594. The play which we know as *2 Henry VI* was entered S.R. March 12, 1594, to T. Millington as "The Firste Parte of the Contention of the twoo famous houses of York and Lancaster," and printed in 1594 by Thomas Creede for Millington, reprinted in 1600 by Valentine Sims for Millington. P[eter] S[hort] had printed *3 Henry VI* (*True Tragedy*) for Thomas Millington in 1595, without known entry, and W.W. had also printed it for Millington in 1600. Millington then transferred both plays to Pavier April 19, 1602, as "The firste and second parte of Henry the Sixt, two bookes."[27] These two plays escaped originally in the spate of plays which had belonged mostly to the complex at the Rose, and were rushing into print in 1593–94. Millington had in some way procured the manuscripts of these two plays, and had produced "bad" quartos. Similarly, it was Creede who procured a manuscript of *Henry V* for a "bad" quarto. If, therefore, a publisher had faulted in procuring copy it was Creede or Millington. Of the three plays, Millington had entered only the first that he published; but his right to both parts, and Creede's right in *Henry V* were recognized by the Stationers' Company in the transfers. Pavier had merely secured the rights of Creede and Millington in the three plays.

These "stolne, and surreptitious copies, maimed, and deformed by the frauds and stealthes of iniurious imposters, that expos'd them" had been printed by Creede in 1594, 1595, and 1600, and Heminges and Cundall were the only surviving "fellowes" of Shakspere from those days before 1594. The fundamental controversy, however, involved the plays of the various "Authors" for the company—as well as for other companies—not merely those of Shakspere. There is also evidence to suggest that some preventive action was taken about 1594, but it does not yet appear who took it and how. The estopping authority could have been the Lord Chamberlain of that day, Henry Carey, Lord Hunsdon, who became patron of Shakspere's company by June 5, 1594. The company then remained the Chamberlain's men, except for some seven months' interregnum of the antagonistic William Brooke, Lord Cobham, till under King James they became the King's Men, though that arrangement still left them actually under the Lord Chamberlain.

But Pavier had no part in this initial procurement of wretched material for "bad" quartos. His claims were from Millington and Creede and were recognized by the Stationers'

27 Greg, *Bibliography*, I, 200–201.   28 Greg, *Bibliography*, III, 1108.

Company as completely legitimate, so far as the brethren were concerned. Not being brethren, if the actors were to seek recourse, it must be through some other authority. So from time to time they appealed to their patron the Lord Chamberlain to help them protect their property rights. Before we examine the Lord Chamberlain's action in 1619, however, we had better let Pavier finish answering briefly the account of his alleged misdeeds.

Pavier we are told, "presumably made some private arrangement with Arthur Johnson and Nathaniel Butter, who were both alive and had valid rights in *The Merry Wives of Windsor* and *King Lear,* since he put their names on the titles."[28] If so, the arrangement was perfectly legal under perfectly legal rights. Of these, *Merry Wives* was correctly dated, but *Lear* misdated, again without rhyme or reason under Sir Walter's explanation, as in the case of Pavier's own plays. But the actors would not have found the "bad" quarto of *Merry Wives* any more to their liking than Pavier's own six plays. Still, on this account Pavier is now justified legally for these two, making eight out of ten cases.

But for the remaining two counts the assumptions are unnecessarily turned against Pavier. "The original owners of *The Merchant of Venice* and *A Midsummer-Night's Dream,* Thomas Hayes and Thomas Fisher, were both dead, and Pavier apparently assumed that their copies were derelict. He took the precaution, however, of ascribing the reprints of these plays to James Roberts, who was also safely dead. It happened, however, that Thomas Hayes had left a son Lawrence, who laid claim to his father's copies, a claim which, so far as *The Merchant of Venice* and one other book were concerned, was allowed by the court of the Stationers' Company on 8 July 1619, by which date we may therefore assume that Pavier's collection had appeared."[29] But why could Pavier not have arranged

29 Greg, *Bibliography,* III, 1108.

with the father before death, or the son after, as legal heir?
Also, Roberts had printed the first quarto of *Merchant of
Venice* in 1600, though Hayes, for whom he printed it, was now
in 1619 dead. Sir Edmund Chambers thinks *Midsummer-
Night's Dream* was derelict. The fact of the business is that we
do not know the details, and the presumption is that Pavier had
in some way acquired as good legal right to publish these four
plays as he had for his own six. The grander rascal we think
him, the more certain we should be that he had protected himself. At any rate, there is no record that any action was taken
against Pavier within the Stationers' Company. As a matter of
fact, he was to become warden, betokening a reputable standing
with the brethren. He had set in motion forces which resulted
in the publication of the First Folio. For this, in charity let us
give him at least one kindly thought.

The actors had in 1619 appealed to the Lord Chamberlain,
and he had taken the action which was open to him. In line with
the tradition of his office from at least 1598, and possibly 1594,
he ordered that no plays of his Majesty's servants should be
printed without their consent. He named no past offender,
though he quoted the actors as to the nature of past offenses,
which are not to occur again. So because of Pavier's enterprise
in 1619, there had in 1619 been a renewal of orders.

When, therefore, *Philaster* was submitted in 1620 for
license, Taverner and the Stationers' Company should certainly
have known that it had been acted by the King's men. Walkley,
at least, advertizes the fact on his title-page. Taverner, as well
as Jaggard, had doubtless assured himself that Walkley was
legally possessed of his particular copy, and that the King's men
would not make trouble. Certainly, so well seasoned a licenser
as Master Taverner would not have risked serious trouble for

30 For further facts on these licenses, see   31 Arnold Glover, *Beaumont and Flet-*
     Appendix.   *cher*, (1905), I, 400.

a license fee, or for any sum Walkley could have offered out of the paltry profits of a play.[30]

Walkley himself did not spare his copy of 1620 or condone its procurers, when in 1622 it was his cue to praise the superiority of the substituted copy. According to his story, the copy of 1620 was "hurt neither by me, nor the Printer," but "maimed and deformed" before it came to them. He had no reason to injure the play, or to permit the printer to do so, and certainly he had observed all the recordable legalities to prove that the copy was his. We wish, of course, that he had told us who did maim and deform the play and how he had procured the resultant copy. All he tells us is in the conventional statement of the title page of 1620 that it was "Acted at the Globe by his Maiesties Seruants." He had entered it properly, and he advertizes that it had belonged to the King's men. He claims, and the facts justify him, that he himself had been guilty of no underhand dealing. The underhand dealing, which he does not in 1622 deny, had been on the part of those from whom he had procured the maimed and deformed copy of the play. In the case of Shakspere's plays, Heminges and Cundall will be more explicit as to how these vendors had faulted.

As to the text of the edition of 1620, "The first few pages and the last few pages of the play as printed in [1620] vary so completely from the other texts that it has been necessary to print them separately."[31] Earlier, Leonhardt had found this first quarto very deficient, though he had noted in its favor the significant fact that it had more precise stage instructions.[32] In respect to its text, the quarto is certainly a bad quarto in spots, and critics appear to accept it even as in parts at least a "bad" bad quarto. But that is not our immediate problem.

While Walkley's blurb was still hot from the press,

32 B. Leonhardt, "Die Textvarienten Von Beaumont und Fletcher's 'Phi-laster'," *Anglia,* XIX, 44.

Heminges and Cundall[33] adopted the figure of curing the wounds of "maimed and deformed" plays so that these could better travel: "copies [which were] maimed and deformed . . . euen those, are now offer'd to your view cur'd, and perfect of their limbes." It is clear that Walkley developed the figure and the climactic epithets out of the sub-title and circumstances of *Philaster* for his "corrected and amended" second edition of 1622. It is equally clear that both the figure and its climactic epithets have been adapted for the prefatory address "To the great Variety of Readers," signed by Heminges and Cundall for the First Folio, entered S.R. November 8, 1623. Since *Philaster* belonged to their company, they would certainly know of Walkley's original venture from maimed and deformed copy in 1620, as well as of his "reformed" copy of 1622. As a matter of fact, where else could Walkley have procured his "reformed" copy?[34] At any rate, Heminges and Cundall knew and borrowed Walkley's figure and epithets of 1622 for their description in 1623 of similar escapees from the Shakspere canon. They were merely elaborating, however, their original objection through the Lord Chamberlain in 1619 that "the bookes [had] much corruption to the iniury and disgrace of the Authors."

Walkley did not say who "maimed and deformed" *Philaster* as published in 1620, further than that neither he nor the printer did it. Nor did he indicate the nature of the maiming. He said nothing either of how he came by the healing copy. Nor do we know how he came by various other King's men plays at this period. Presumably the adjudication, formal or informal, which must have followed upon the renewed order of 1619 recognized his right in these, and the King's men would pre-

---

33 There is no guarantee, of course, that Heminges and Cundall actually wrote the blurb which is authenticated by their names. But if in any sense or degree they had a ghost writer, he was already a captive ghost by 1619, and had peeped over the shoulders of various interesting persons associated with the company before he produced his masterpiece of 1623. At least, he chose always to manifest himself in connection with "the players."

34 Henry Smith complained "To the Reader" of his *Wedding Garment*

sumably have cooperated like sensible men, as in the case of the First Folio, wherever it was for them the most satisfactory way out.

But however it came about, it is clear that Heminges and Cundall have adapted Walkley's conceit to describe a whole group of escapees from the Shakspere canon, which were "stolne, and surreptitious copies, maimed, and deformed by the frauds and stealthes of iniurious impostors, that expos'd them." Even without Walkley's disclaimer to guide us, and the earlier protest in 1619 at the "much corruption," it must be directly evident that Heminges and Cundall are not referring here to either publishers or printers. Obviously, a publisher would prefer his plays unmaimed and undeformed, and even the printer would rather have a clean manuscript—to begin with! Heminges and Cundall reprehend no printer or publisher in their condemnation of these "maimed, and deformed" plays as a class but the impostors who, having stolen, by stealth exposed the plays thus "maimed, and deformed." In looking all these years for printers and publishers to blame we have certainly been wrong. For all Heminges and Cundall have to say, all these printers and publishers (pirates, no less, every mother's son of them! And upon occasion about everybody else! Diogenes could have saved his labor there!) may have been as lilly-fingered as Walkley claims he and his printer were. After all, it was in succession to the rights established by the publishers of the execrated copy in the bad quartos that the authentic forms were now being printed, just as in the case of Walkley and *Philaster*.

We must note now that Heminges and Cundall claimed

(1590) that it had been procured from notes, and "because they had gotten it licensed before" they were about to print it, so he supplied a good copy, and "suffered that which I could not hinder." The authors and owners of plays would find them-

selves in the same position. If the publisher had a copy, good or bad, and procured a license, then the outsider had no recourse through the Stationers' Company. He could not even go to another publisher with a good copy.

also to have produced "all the rest, absolute in their numbers, as
he conceiued thē." Here we need to consider two other statements in 1623 concerning plays for the King's men, previously
unprinted. *The Duchess of Malfy* (not entered) claims on its
title-page to be "The perfect and exact Coppy, with diuerse
things Printed, that the length of the Play would not beare in
the Presentment." *The Devils Law Case* (not entered) claims
on its title-page to be "The true and perfect Copie from the
Originall." Since Webster, the author, had a hand in the publication of both his plays, he is evidently responsible directly or
indirectly for the insistence upon "perfect Copie" from the uncut original, which, of course, he would have written and so
could guarantee. Why these plays were not entered does not
appear. Nor what the King's men thought of Webster's publishing plays they had bought from him. Jonson had, of course,
published his plays for the King's men as openly as did Webster.
Here we simply do not know the arrangements.

Before this group of plays in 1622–23 for the King's men,
it had been the custom to advertize that the play was printed
"as it was acted." But in 1622 Walkley used the epithets
"maimed and deformed" to describe the previous edition of
Philaster, and in 1623 Heminges and Cundall adapted the terms
to stigmatize the poor quartos. Webster, on the other hand, had
insisted in 1623 on the perfect and exact uncut original of the
author. So Heminges and Cundall insisted that these plays of
Shakspere were "absolute in their numbers, as he conceiued
thē." As we shall see, Humphrey Mosely understood Heminges and Cundall here to be alluding to the same thing as
Webster. Whether for Beaumont and Fletcher, Webster, or
Shakspere, the insistence in 1622–23 was that these plays for
the King's men were from the complete and uncut originals,
accurately transcribed. But in each case Shakspere was the
residuary legatee. The original statements were not made

directly to fit his case, but were adapted to it later, a fact which raises the question of how well they were adapted.

It should not be overlooked, however, that this shift in emphasis in 1622–23 to the true and perfect original correlates exactly with the shift in editorial policy for the First Folio. The comedies had been edited in 1621 and 1622 with emphasis upon secondary stage-types of manuscript, but the histories and tragedies in 1622–23 with emphasis upon the author's original or on unimproved stage copy. It is this second and final view which finds expression in the statements borrowed and bettered for Heminges and Cundall in 1623. It would be of fundamental importance to know exactly how this shift in the editorial policy for the First Folio came about. If we knew who actually garnered the ideas subscribed by Heminges and Cundall, we should probably have unriddled that problem. The same person was certainly closely connected with all these instances. Being the author, Webster naturally insisted in his own person. Had he any further connection with shaping the editorial policy of the First Folio? I merely ask the question.

As is well known, when Humphrey Moseley came to write from "The Stationer to the Readers" for the First Folio of Beaumont and Fletcher, 1647, he "cut over the pattern" of the similar letter of Heminges and Cundall to the First Folio of Shakspere, and thereby indicates how he understood some of its terms. Heminges and Cundall had exhorted the reader that since the author of these plays is dead, "do not envie his Friends, the office of their care, and paine, to haue collected & publish'd them." Moseley likewise emphasizes his pains in collecting and printing all the genuine unprinted plays of Beaumont and Fletcher, except *The Wild Goose Chase,* which could not be located.

Heminges and Cundall had continued, "and so to haue publish'd them, as where (before) you were abus'd with diuerse stolne, and surreptitious copies, maimed, and deformed by the frauds and stealthes of iniurious impostors, that expos'd them: euen those, are now offer'd to your view cur'd, and perfect of their limbes; and all the rest, absolute in their numbers, as he conceiued thē." Similarly Moseley explains that he has not included previously printed plays, since the readers would already have them, the implication being that these were satisfactory. But some would have memories or even written copies of the plays he prints. So, "One thing I must answer before it bee objected; 'tis this: When these *Comedies* and *Tragedies* were presented on the Stage, the *Actours* omitted some *Scenes* and Passages (with the *Authour's* consent) as occasion led them; and when private friends desir'd a Copy, they then (and justly too) transcribed what they *Acted*. But now you have both All that was *Acted,* and all that was not; even the perfect full Originalls without the least mutilation; So that were the *Authours* living, (and sure they can never dye) they themselves would challenge neither more nor lesse then what is here published; this Volume being now so compleate and finish'd, that the Reader must expect no future Alterations." Moseley has besides done all he could to avoid the *"literall Errours* committed by the Printer," sparing no costs and pains to get these "free and unmangled" copies from widely dispersed sources. He has searched out and paid for the perfect full originals, "free and unmangled," in contradistinction to the copies stigmatized by Heminges and Cundall as emanating from "impostors," who pretended ownership but had only "stolne and surreptitious copies" which they had procured by "frauds and stealthes."

Heminges and Cundall had continued of Shakspere, "who, as he was a happie imitator of Nature, was a most gentle expresser of it. His mind and hand went together: And what he thought, he vttered with that easinesse, that wee haue scarse receiued from him a blot in his papers." Similarly, Moseley concludes, "What ever I have seene of Mr. *Fletchers* owne hand, is free from interlining; and his friends affirme he never writ any one thing twice: it seemes he had that rare felicity to prepare and perfect all first in his owne braine; to shape and attire his *Notions,* to adde or loppe off, before he committed one word to writing, and never touched pen till all was to stand as firme and immutable as if ingraven in Brasse or Marble." Incidentally, the implication is that these plays were not all in Fletcher's hand, and the impression from "Whatever I have seene of Mr. *Fletchers* owne hand" is that few, if any, of them were.

Moseley claims to have used "even the perfect full Originalls without the least mutilation," "free and unmangled," not such manuscripts as were cut for the stage. These stage copies are thus stigmatized indirectly as mutilated and mangled, particularly the copies from stage copies for private friends. Anyone who has examined such cut stage copies attentively, say the two for Cartwright,[35] which were made upon print, after scenery demanded even more drastic cutting to conserve time, will know what a mutilated and mangled mess of a text resulted when the original was edited to the stage. Only stage devotees with their hearts set upon acting could prefer these—quite correctly! For literary purposes, however, certainly one would far prefer the uncut, unmutilated, unmangled originals, even if they also were in something of a mess. Moseley had no doubt about this for his readers, as Heminges and Cundall had none for theirs, nor Walkley for his, nor Webster and Brome as authors for theirs, *ad infinitum.*

If any of the plays of Beaumont and Fletcher had already been published from such stage copies, Moseley gives no hint, but instead indirectly approves these already printed plays, since he does not propose to print better forms. But Heminges and Cundall stigmatize some of the previous publications as from

35 See G. B. Evans, *Plays and Poems of William Cartwright,* pp. 260–61.

"diuerse stolne, and surreptitious copies, maimed, and deformed by the frauds and stealthes of iniurious impostors, that expos'd them." "Euen those, are now offer'd to your view cur'd, and perfect of their limbes; and all the rest, absolute in their numbers, as he conceiued thē," his papers having been without blot. Their words suggested to Moseley the copies mutilated and mangled from the author's original for stage purposes, for Moseley himself had no such problem. He brings it in here by contrast only because his models Heminges and Cundall had been obliged to face it. He is adapting to his authors both the condemnation and the praise of Heminges and Cundall, who were themselves here echoing Webster's disclaimer of such cut forms.

It will be noticed that in 1647 Moseley assumed that for the plays of Beaumont and Fletcher, extending back well into the first decade of the century, "the *Actours* omitted some *Scenes* and Passages (with the *Authour's* consent) as occasion led them." The Title to *The Duchess of Malfy* had implied this in 1623, "The perfect and exact Coppy with diuerse things Printed, that the length of the Play would not beare in the Presentment." It must be evident that authors would be somewhat less than enthusiastic over the necessary addition and lopping, to use Moseley's words, of the author's own composition by the mere mechanicals as they fitted the art of a play to the Procrustean bed of the stage. Says Brome, *Antipodes,* 1638, "You shal find in this Booke more then was presented upon the *Stage,* and left out of the *Presentation,* for superfluous length (as some of the *Players* pretended) [.] I thoght good al should be inserted according to the allowed *Original;* and as it was, at first, intended for the *Cock-pit Stage*."[36] As early as 1600, Brome's master, one Benjamin Jonson, had advertized upon the title-page of *Every Man Out,* "Containing more than

36 Greg, *Bibliography,* III, 1226–27. Notice that the actors cut the "allowed

hath been Publickely Spoken or Acted," though he does not say whether the actors cut or he added.

Cutting and editing for the stage was thus an established part of the play routine. The question of why dramatists writing to order wilfully wrote more than could be acted has no bearing here. The established fact is that they did, and that, even contrary to their own judgment, their work would be cut and adapted to the stage. In fact, it is correct to say that the actors cut the play (by Caesarean operation as it were) out of the author's original, whether before or after it had been allowed. For the play as play, the actors and their employees were responsible, not the author. They shaped his ends, rough-hew them how he would. As actor, Shakspere might have been a bit more canny than other authors, but we shall not be wise to assume it without proof. There is always the great law of laziness; why do for yourself what someone else will do for you? And Shakspere has been thoroughly convicted as in some things having a positive genius for laziness.

It is clear and generally accepted that one thing wrong with "poor" quartos is that they are from cut copies, mutilated and mangled, usually even more severely "maimed and deformed" than Moseley implies, or surviving manuscripts indicate, was normal. This Heminges and Cundall imply in their terms of condemnation; these cut, mutilated, and mangled copies were not even honest ghosts, but had been further dishonested by the method of procurement.

Enough is now known about the texts of the First Folio to make it certain that Heminges and Cundall were at least as precise in their statements as were Walkley, Webster, and Moseley. All were advertizing blithely in the ballyhoo of their own times, and to their own times, without any thought of the cross-questioning, and lie-detector tests modern scholars would

Original."

put them through. They did in effect reject all previous quartos, good or bad, as they imply, for I believe it is agreed that in every case of a preceding quarto they either substituted a manuscript, or they used the most readily available "good" quarto, whether the "best" as we might think or not, checked in some degree to some manuscript. No quarto was ever the standard, but the manuscript to which it was checked. The extent to which some quartos were used even as agents of transcription is still being called into question and in some cases may well be found to have been exaggerated by past opinion. But such use of a quarto would have saved a great deal of time in the process of furnishing what the actors regarded as authentic copy, even if it did prevent our getting sight of the complete manuscripts, especially the details of them. More than half of the plays not previously printed show the characteristic acts and scenes of an author's original. Only in a few cases, if any, can the actors have used cut versions. But to insist that they claim to have printed in any instance directly from an actual manuscript which Shakspere had dashed off in his own handwriting without a blot is simply to display ignorance of the rhetorical habits of the time. The meaning of their rhetoric can be derived only from a knowledge of the actual facts which it attempts in elevated terms to suggest. The facts form the Rosetta stone for interpretation of their language, not any logical or philological meanings we would impose as our personal impressions upon their words.

As Sir Walter Greg has put the case, "It has been argued, cogently enough so far as logic is concerned, that these words, to have any significance, must be taken to apply not to a fair copy even autograph, but to the original drafts themselves. Certainly the textual and bibliographical critic of Shakespeare is bound to ask himself whether they do, and if so whether they are true. I do not pretend to know the answer, but I think the parallel case of Fletcher deserves consideration, and certainly a good deal of recent criticism of Shakespeare's text assumes a pretty sweeping negative."[37] In the years since Sir Walter wrote that statement, his own work and that of others have made the negative even more sweeping.

37 Greg, *Dramatic Documents,* p. 197.

Chapter Ten

SHAKSPERE'S AUTOGRAPH

HAVE WE finally discovered the direct highway to Shak-spere's autograph? Not even a bypath. At best, we have merely escaped from a few blind alleys, and may, I hope, now avoid a few more. On the main point, we are not appreciably less igno-rant than Pope and Dr. Johnson; we merely have a fuller knowledge of the extent of our ignorance. Fortunately, we have a voluminous anatomy of our present state in the work of Sir Walter Greg.

We shall need first to see how Sir Walter has arrived at his major classifications into prompt-books and foul papers, which are not exclusive of each other. For "foul papers come somehow into the picture in the case of twenty-five plays, and a prompt-book in the case of twenty-one;"[1] that is, about half of the "prompt-books" are connected with "foul papers," a propor-tion which arouses no statistical suspicions. Sir Walter is thus driving a double team, each of which we must try out separately.

Sir Walter's classifications are entirely inferential, without any attempt to derive them historically from actual known instances, though the known historical instances are in the back-ground. Sir Walter begins at the source with the author's own copy or copies, where our inferences are necessarily theoretical entirely, since actually we have no manuscript for Shakspere. "Obviously the type of manuscript that first presents itself for consideration is the author's rough draft of his play, the 'foul

1 Greg, *First Folio*, p. 430.

sheets' mentioned by Daborne, the 'foul papers' we shall find Edward Knight transcribing. By a rough draft is not to be understood a first sketch but a copy representing the play more or less as the author intended it to stand, but not itself clear or tidy enough to serve as a prompt-book. Whether behind it lay a rougher draft we can hardly tell. In some cases it is probable enough; but an experienced dramatist would doubtless be able to produce at once a sufficiently coherent text."[2]

Consequently, the distinction between foul papers and prompt-copy is entirely inferential, with practically no known instances to guide us. "Characteristic of foul papers are, first of all, loose ends and false starts and unresolved confusions in the text, which sometimes reveal themselves as duplications in print: next, inconsistency in the designation of characters in directions and prefixes alike, and occasionally the substitution of the name of an actor, when the part is written with a particular performer in view:[3] lastly, the appearance of indefinite and permissive stage-directions, and occasionally of explanatory glosses on the text. It must, however, be recognized that owing to the casual ways of book-keepers these characteristics may persist, to some extent at least, in the prompt-book; but in general the ordering of the text seems to have received more attention than that of the directions, which was perhaps only natural. Characteristic of prompt-copy are the appearance of actors' names duplicating those of (usually minor) characters, possibly the general appearance of directions a few lines too early, and warnings for actors or properties to be in readiness. At the same time these features may be introduced by the book-keeper into the foul papers if he annotates them with a view to transcription. The possibility may not be a very serious one, but it should none the less be borne in mind. It may be added, however, that whatever deductions have to be made from the weight of these criteria,

2 Greg, *First Folio,* p. 106.   4 Greg, *First Folio,* p. 142.
3 See below, pp. 146–48.

the presence of any of them in a print argues a close dependence
on a playhouse manuscript of some sort, which carries with it a
high degree of authority."[4] One very fundamental difficulty
about this theoretical reasoning is that to be worth much it
must assume a normal routine, whereas the surviving evidence
at most indicates individual habits. By the twenties of the
seventeenth century, routines were beginning to be established,
but the nineties of the sixteenth century had at best not gone as
far.

Since we have approached from the point of view of
surviving "prompt-books," as they are differentiated by Sir
Walter, how do these three proposed criteria correlate with our
findings? The first characteristic is "the appearance of actors'
names duplicating those of (usually minor) characters." Sir
Edmund Chambers lists these plays as "*2, 3 Hen. VI, Tam. of
Shrew, Rom. & Jul., Mid. N. Dr., 2 Hen. IV, Hen. V, Much
Ado, All's Well.*"[5] In the First Folio, three of these (*2* and *3
Henry VI, Romeo*) are undivided; five (*Shrew,* imperfectly;
Dream, Henry V, irregularly; *Ado, Well*) are in acts; only one,
2 Henry IV, is in acts and scenes. But *2 Henry IV* had been
first printed in undivided quarto, with the actors' names already
there. So had *Ado,* with the names of Kempe and Cowley im-
bedded in it, while in the First Folio "Iacke Wilson" gets
added. *Dream,* too, had been printed in an undivided "good"
quarto, but no actor is named in that. Basically, therefore, five
of these plays (*2* and *3 Henry VI, Romeo, 2 Henry IV, Ado*)
are from undivided stage copies. Two (*Dream, Well*) are in
acts in the First Folio, though *Dream* was undivided in its
"good" quarto. *Shrew* is imperfectly in acts, and *Henry V* irregularly so. Thus all plays with actors' names, being nine out
of thirty-six, one-fourth of the plays in the First Folio, belong
to the second class, the majority of them entirely undivided,

5 Chambers, *William Shakespeare,* I, 237, n. 2.

only two being fully divided even into acts, and one of these with a preceding undivided quarto. This wholly objective characteristic belongs entirely within our second class, mostly to undivided plays, such as were characteristic of the stage copies of the nineties. Since technically *2 Henry IV* is of the first class, eight of the seventeen plays of the second class, nearly half, have actors' names.

Further, the actors named in the seven undivided or not completely divided plays belong to the nineties, while those in the two divided plays belong around 1620, in *Dream* around 1620, in *Well* probably around 1620 but possibly as early as the first decade of the seventeenth century.[6] The addition of "Iacke Wilson" in the folio version of *Ado* (divided into acts) evidently belongs also around 1620. That is, the undivided plays are from stage copies of the nineties, and those divided into acts, the stage copies of the seventeenth century, around 1620. The correlation with our findings from surviving materials of this class is exact and complete, where we found that stage copies of the nineties were undivided, but those of the seventeenth century noted acts in the margin.[7]

While this characteristic does appear in the undivided stage copies of the nineties, there is an unusually heavy incidence in the printed plays of Shakspere. Some printed plays outside of Shakspere do preserve the names of actors, but the number so far located is small, being more for Shakspere than for all the remainder of Elizabethan drama. The characteristic may prove to be peculiar to a period, or to a company, even to some individual official. Or it may be that Heminges and Cundall simply considered this kind of manuscript to be the most authentic available for these particular plays.

There has, however, been some division of opinion as to

6 See Baldwin, *Organization and Personnel, passim.*

7 In the case of *Woodstock* and *Iron-* sides, the seventeenth-century additions were made on undivided stage-copy of the early type. Cf. *Ado.*

whether all these jottings of actors' names belong to a stage-reviser, or some of them to Shakspere himself. Crompton Rhodes and Professor Allison Gaw had independently hit upon the idea that Shakspere himself had inserted the names of some of these actors. Sir Edmund Chambers rejected the notion. "But the book-keeper is clearly revealed in several places where the printer has preserved the name of an actor written beside or in substitution for that of the character which he played. Generally this occurs in stage-directions, and the analogy of the theatrical manuscripts rules out the alternative explanation of Professor Gaw, who finds here the mind of Shakespeare unconsciously identifying the part with the personality of its representative. The case is perhaps not so simple where, as in *Much Ado About Nothing,* the actor-names run through a series of speech-prefixes. But probably Shakespeare wrote inadequate prefixes, in the form of mere numerals, and the book-keeper glossed them.[8] A guard must be kept against the attempts of Fleay and others to find the names of actors in those assigned textually to servants and other members of crowds. The book-keeper could have no occasion to trouble about textual names, and the author, writing in advance of casting, would certainly not know to whom such small parts would be given."[9]

Following down his theory of authorial inconsistencies and idiosyncrasies, Dr. McKerrow had also developed this idea, that since the author knew the actors he is likely the person in certain cases who has inserted the names, and Sir Walter Greg in his pursuit of "foul papers" has championed McKerrow against Chambers, pointing out that "we need to distinguish two quite different ways in which [these inserted names] occur."[10] The distinction is entirely theoretical so far as origins

8. For the probable explanation, see Baldwin, *Organization and Personnel,* p. 302.

9 Chambers, *William Shakespeare,* I, 237.

10 Greg, *First Folio,* p. 114.

are concerned, as Sir Edmund has pointed out. Sir Walter continues, "To this theory it has been objected that in the manuscripts that have come down to us actors' names occur exclusively as additions by the book-keeper, and Chambers considers this decisive. It is, however, sufficient to point out in reply that in any case the authorial use of actors' names would be exceptional, that they would very likely not survive beyond the foul papers, and that our extant playhouse manuscripts are mostly prompt-books."[11] This reply admits that there are no facts to substantiate the theory, but proffers other theories which are themselves unsubstantiated by any surviving fact. The fundamental fact is that in known surviving manuscripts for the stage, insertion of the name of an actor is done always by some official of the company, never by the author.

Independently of all these, in a work which went to press in June 1925, I arrived at essentially the same conclusions and on the same grounds of fact as did Sir Edmund Chambers several years later.[12] I did not then see anything in the organization and personnel of Shakspere's company to indicate that Shakspere had initially anything to do with these insertions of actors' names, and now upward of forty years later, without controverting facts, I am of the same opinion still, especially now in view of the type to which the plays themselves belong. But whether these jottings of actors' names were made by Shakspere or by some stage-reviser has no bearing upon the fact that these nine plays, one-fourth of the plays in the First Folio, belong to one type of stage copy, characteristic of the nineties, and but slightly adapted in the seventeenth century, *Ado* showing both the original form and the seventeenth century adaptation.

As we have seen above,[13] such jottings of actors' names might also occur on theatrical plots, and it is an important corollary for such plays that where the jottings are due to a

11 Greg, *First Folio*, p. 116.   *nel*, pp. 137ff.
12 Baldwin, *Organization and Person-*   13 See above, p. 38.

stage-reviser, it was not the intention to use this stage copy with a theatrical plot.

Besides actors' names, Sir Walter gives two other possible criteria for prompt-copy, "possibly the general appearance of directions a few lines too early, and warnings for actors or properties to be in readiness." If Sir Walter has examined these characteristics systematically, I have not located the results. But, at least in one instance, an anticipatory entrance disturbs him. Sir Walter wishes *Julius Caesar* to join peaceably six other plays and be an "official" prompt-book. "The anticipatory entry of a character can be paralleled in several plays apparently printed from his foul papers. . . . There is one difficulty in supposing that F was printed from a normal prompt-book, namely that we should hardly expect the book-keeper in preparing it to have transcribed the sometimes redundant directions of the author, or to have repeated in the margin directions he had already written elsewhere."[14] To these recalcitrances we must add the objective fact that *Julius Caesar* is divided only into acts, not into acts and scenes, as are the other six "official" plays. *Julius Caesar* does not belong to the first class, but to the second, and the characteristics objected to by Sir Walter add it to our nine plays which had actors' names. This case and Sir Walter's cautious "possibly" on the characteristic involved should warn us that it would be difficult to get an objective statement, as we can on actors' names. And this is not the place to attempt another complete review of the evidence play by play.

On other grounds, Sir Walter considers that "A prompt-book of some sort lies behind . . . *Titus Andronicus* (in the shape of a quarto) . . . and some reference was made to it in connexion with . . . *The Merchant of Venice*."[15] In the First Folio, these plays are of the second class, though *Titus*

14 Greg, *First Folio*, p 291.   15 Greg, *First Folio*, p. 430.

had an undivided quarto. If these two are also accepted, we shall have twelve plays of our second class connected with stage copy, though one of these, *2 Henry IV*, is technically of the first class, thus leaving eleven out of the seventeen plays of the second class. The other six (*Errors, Labour's Lost, Troilus, Coriolanus, Timon, Antony*) may or may not also be from stage copy. For these external chance characteristics might very readily fail to get recorded in print, especially if the manuscript was lightly marked, and for the most part as usual in the left margin. After all, these characteristics are complete externalities to the text and evidently could be recorded on any available manuscript. They have no necessary correlation, therefore, with the fundamental text to which they may be applied. And their survival in printed texts was not in the first instance desired, but more or less accidental. When any or all of these characteristics do not appear in print we cannot be certain from that fact alone that any or all of them were not in the parent manuscript. The stage-reviser merely jotted down a few things on which he did not trust his memory. Nor was there any reason why these should be preserved in print further than the fact of their existence—unless indeed some editor fell in love with them, which is not likely.

The most significant fact emerging from our examination is that nine plays containing actors' names all belong basically to the second class, mostly undivided; that is, to the type of stage copy prevalent in the nineties, and reflected in the "good" quartos. Also, the correlation and variation, according to whether a "good" quarto agrees with a manuscript of the first or with one of the second class shows pragmatically that this distinction into classes as derived from actual surviving "prompt-books" is valid. This fact in turn puts the quartos as a class in their places. The authorities thought they had checked the texts of these to better manuscripts for the Folio text. It is thus those better manuscripts which become our standards unless we know better than the selecting authorities, not either quarto or Folio, as seems too regularly, at least tacitly, to be assumed. It is still important to know the file of quartos, since the first in the sequence is also close to some manuscript, and conceivably others might have direct connections in some respects. But for the manuscripts selected as the "best" available for the Folio text, the quarto actually used is the significant one. Where a manuscript of the second class was used for the text of the Folio, the quarto and Folio corroborate each other, since they trace eventually to the same manuscript, but that manuscript was usually a stage-copy, not Shakspere's autograph directly. Where a manuscript of the first class was used for the text of the Folio, the genuine changes from the quarto take precedence, and the question is how thoroughly and correctly the quarto has been checked to the manuscript, if it was so checked. Shakspere's autograph could be involved directly here; at worst a direct descendant which was considered to be the best available. Where there is no quarto, we face the two types directly to see what they are.

But at least we now have a historical frame of reference for criticizing plays of the second class, especially those that had early "good" quartos. We need to interpret them in the light of the stage copies of the nineties. Though they were stage copies, they were early stage copies, and those that were published in early "good" quartos had not yet suffered the possible depredations of two or three decades. They should be accepted and evaluated for what they actually are, not Shakspere's autograph indeed, but stage copies, no doubt reasonably close in the text to Shakspere's own autograph. It is doubtless significant that Sir Walter Greg classifies the "good" quartos generally as from Shakspere's "foul" papers.

So much for our second class. But what of the first? Sir Walter groups six, or one-third of the plays of this class, as having "the official prompt-book behind them"[16] (*Gentlemen, Wives, Like It, Night, Macbeth, Cymbeline*). He also includes *Julius Caesar*, of the second class, which we have seen fit to remove. It is important to see how Sir Walter has arrived at this grouping, and again it is not by comparison historically with surviving "official" "prompt-books," as he has himself determined them. Here we come to Sir Walter's primary criterion, which proves to be relative "fairness" or "foulness." It will be remembered that his primary division is a squinting one of twenty-one texts from prompt-copies and twenty-five from foul papers. Out of this mass, he then winnows his seven (our six) "official" prompt-books. He finds that the fourteen "good" quartos and eleven of the texts first printed in the First Folio are from "foul papers," a total of twenty-five. This leaves eleven plays first printed in the First Folio as not from "foul papers," and consequently the only ones which may be from "fair" copies. Of the eleven, four more are dropped, apparently because of irregularity in act and scene-division, for *John* and *1 Henry VI* are irregular in acts and scenes, while *2* and *3 Henry VI* are undivided. This leaves seven, which we have reduced to six.

The reason for the regularity and "fairness" of these six plays is readily apparent. Four of the six (*Gentlemen, Wives, Like It, Night*) are comedies. Two of the four (*Gentlemen, Night*) belong to Dr. McKerrow's group of plays with excessively regular speech-headings, while two (*Gentlemen, Wives*) are Crane copies. We have seen reason to agree with Dr. McKerrow that a play with excessive regularity in speech-headings "is more likely to have been printed from some sort of fair copy, perhaps made by a professional scribe"; and to agree with Sir Walter Greg and apparently everybody else that Crane was the professional scribe concerned in two of these plays. Crane's work was evidently done for the First Folio. It follows

---

16 Greg, *First Folio*, p. 429.

that his part of the regularizing was done about 1621. It would
not follow that he also regularized the stage characteristics of
three (*Gentlemen*, *Wives*, *Night*) out of our four comedies
at the same time; for a "fair" copy with most of these characteristics could have been made at any time. As we have seen,
Crane copied *Gentlemen* and *Wives*. There was at least a
possible occasion for someone to make a "fair" copy of *Night*
about this period, since it was performed at Court on Easter
Monday 1618, and again February 2, 1623.[17] But there is no
record of acting at this period for *Like It*, as there is none
for *Gentlemen* and *Wives*. Regularity is not likely to have been
thrust upon these four comedies solely because of revival at
this time, though revival could have played some part. In view
of what we already know about three of the four comedies, we
probably had better generalize Dr. McKerrow's principle into,
"a play in which [external characteristics] are regular and uniform is more likely to have been printed from some sort of
fair copy, perhaps made by a professional scribe," and permit
Sir Walter to account for his group of six (though not seven)
plays as "fair" copies, perhaps professionally made. But at least
two of the copies were made for the First Folio, whether they
were regularized at that time or not, and there is no external
evidence that the others were made "fair" for stage purposes.
Nor is it alleged that the group shows the characteristics of
surviving "Prompt-Books" of the twenties. So far as I can
see, the group has not been arrived at by any positive criteria,
but by elimination in the first place from irregular "foul copies," and by contra-distinctive "regularity" in the second. I
would prefer, therefore, to go no further than to say that they
are probably "fair" copies, to some extent regularized. If these
"fair" copies were not made specifically for the First Folio, one
would suppose that they were at some time made for some stage

17 Chambers, *William Shakespeare*, II, 346.

purposes, but I find no evidence to indicate that they were "official" "Prompt-Books."

Besides these six plays from the "official" prompt-books, Sir Walter in one way and another would connect all plays of our first class with some kind of prompt-book except *Tempest*, *Measure*, *Tale*, *1 Henry IV*, and *Henry VIII*. We cannot here examine his reasons in detail. But Sir Walter's findings supplement and support our two classes derived from actual surviving "Prompt-Books," as delimited by Greg himself.

These texts of the first class, being in acts and scenes, should derive this characteristic from Shakspere's autograph, without editorial interference. If they were from prompt-copy, as Sir Walter thinks most, or all, of them are, then in this respect they are intended to be faithful copies of Shakspere's autograph. But with chastened spirit we should remember at once what with the best of intentions was done to at least five of the seven comedies of the first class; we editors simply must improve; that is our divine mission in life. Such knowledge, therefore, as we have acquired here on the process merely improves our ignorance on the fundamental. We are still where we have always been, seeking light on the individual case, and that alone is really worth anything.

And as a parting shot we should also point out as emphatically as possible that while all the plays of the Folio conform in their divisions to the characteristics of one type or the other of "Prompt-Books," that fact is in itself no guarantee that actually they are from "Prompt-Books." They simply conform to the types, and if they are from stage copies at all are likely from some form of prompt-book, as other characteristics in the majority of cases confirm. But the matter of division, by which we have classified principally, goes back in one form or another to the author, and so could be from a nonstage copy emanating from the author.

Sir Walter thinks, however, that we may rule out non-playhouse manuscripts, at least for the plays first printed in the Folio. "Of the thirty-six plays in the Folio, twenty-two were printed there for the first time, at any rate in a reputable text, and in each instance from a playhouse manuscript. Fourteen plays had previously appeared in what commonly pass for 'good' quartos, and all these probably were used as copy for the Folio. But only ten of them had been printed from regular playhouse manuscripts. Two, *Troilus and Cressida* and *Othello*, had been printed from private transcripts, but while that of *Troilus* had been made, with some correction, by the author himself and was in consequence of particularly high authority, that of *Othello* was less trustworthy. The quartos of *Richard III* and *King Lear*, whatever their precise origin, contained manifestly corrupt texts. Of these facts the editors were fully aware, and they only allowed these four quartos to be used after they had been diligently compared with manuscripts in the theatre. Even some of the other quartos they only approved after similar comparison had been made. While, therefore, it is certain that many errors of one sort and another found their way into the Folio, no less certain is the general authority of the sources on which it drew. In eight cases the text was probably printed direct from Shakspere's autograph copy, in another eleven cases from a quarto that had in its turn been so printed."[18] For the details, we will permit the great authority of Sir Walter to be responsible. At least, his findings do not disturb our findings (though ours disturb his at places), and if true support them.

The stigmata by which we determine prompt-copy are essentially external, thrust in or on the play by some stage-reviser as he prepared the author's text, including stage-directions, for acting. In actual surviving "Prompt-Books" the stage-revisers show little interest in the text itself. They do not edit the text of the author's autograph further than is necessary superficially

18 Greg, *First Folio*, pp. 430–31.

to cut, shape, and adapt it to the stage. They show no literary or even regularizing ambitions. In fact, most of them need to be regularized themselves, though each has his characteristic habits. If the surviving nonautograph "Prompt-Books" have been regularized or otherwise improved in form or content, that was done before or in copying, by the copyist or by someone preparing the materials for him to copy. The stage-adapter therefore, as such, was not offended with the author's fairness or foulness. So far as he was concerned, the author's text might stand in all its foul glory.

This brings us to Sir Walter's second classification, "foul papers." It will be at once evident that the two classes of "Prompt-Books" which we have established know nothing of actual "foul papers" as such. For we have only one play, *Bonduca*, which is said to be from "fowle papers," though others are foul enough to be suspected. In this copy, how much edited we do not know, "There is a division in the manuscript into acts only (whereas the folio marks scenes as well) but in each case the heading includes mention of the first scene."[19] This copy from "fowle papers" belongs to our second class, whereas the folio, which also must be descended from these same "fowle papers" or from still "fouler" ones, is of the first class. The "fowle papers" of *Bonduca* may thus have been either of the first or of the second class—or for that matter undivided. We simply do not have a single known conclusive case of "foul papers" so far as division is concerned.

As Sir Walter knows, he is not reasoning in terms of actual theatrical "foul papers" at all, for we do not have such. Rather he deduces that certain forms of inconsistent imperfection belong to the author, and consequently he must assume that those should have been cleaned up in the "fair" copy which the author turned in, or which someone else made. So far as Shakspere himself is concerned, the evident answer of the twenty-one plays

19 Greg, *Dramatic Documents*, p. 322.

which Sir Walter himself connects with prompt-copy is that the underlying manuscripts had not been fully cleaned up. If they had been, we would not have these imperfections. Shakspere's own "fair" copies for these plays; that is, the copies with which he was permitted to stop his part of the operations, were evidently this "foul." "Foul is fair, and fair is foul." The fundamental difficulty is that papers which the author handed in are sometimes spoken of as "foul," at other times as "fair." There may, of course, be an actual distinction; but until we are better informed, it might be best to use some more neutral term or terms for the author's product, rserving "fair" for the professional copy. The important thing after all is authenticity, not whether the copies should be labeled "fair" or "foul." In its origins all composition is more or less "foul," and lucky as well as hardworking is he who can eliminate all foulness from his fair form. For general sloppiness, Shakspere's "fair" copies can hardly have been any worse than Heywood's autograph *Captives*, which is and must be classed as a "Prompt-Book," even though we hope someone was to make a fair copy of it if it was to be used for actual prompting.

It is thus apparent that to prove that a play is from a "Prompt-Book" is not to prove that it has divested itself of all characteristics of the author's "foul papers." No beneficent stage-reviser is known to have bestowed such perfection upon anyone—for that, let us be thankful! The editor or editors for the "Prompt-Book" simply did their work, fair or foul, upon the given manuscript, autograph or copy, whether it was completely fair or relatively foul. All depends upon the standard demanded of and maintained by an author for the fair copies he handed in. And the standard for Shakspere is not likely to have been equally high or even the same throughout his working days. The early conditions particularly are likely to have permitted only lax work. Custom may have tamed him into more orderly ways; but, on the other hand, familiarity may have bred such contempt of routines that he "got away with" all that prestige could dare. These are things to be discovered, not to be inferred. For instance, since twelve of the undivided quartos are as a class assigned to "foul papers," and since we have seen that they belong to an early type of stage manuscript, we evidently need to find out as exactly as possible why in this type of stage manuscript there was less editorial interference for the "Prompt-Book." Had this editorial interference already functioned before the copy was made, to what extent, by whom, where and how recorded, etc.?

Prompt copies and foul papers are thus by no means mutually exclusive, and the idea behind "foul papers" is likely to be a very fruitful one, since it centers attention upon Shakspere himself, though we might better rechristen it, so as to avoid entangling connotations. Certainly also, under the conditions as known, the author himself is the person first to be suspected in the case of faulty workmanship. According to their lights, others would in their various ways improve the author's work for their purposes. But there is little in surviving instances to indicate that any of these felt called upon to any considerable degree to improve the author's fundamental structure and rhetoric. The editing was for other purposes. We can, therefore, hope pretty well to remove these encrusting improvements, and justly to leave the residual errors to Shakspere. But they should be left as errors, not excused and obscured by "improvement."

We are in danger, however, of attributing every real or fancied foulness to Shakspere, when we know in some respects he must have had various able assistants. Parallels always prove too much, and one can never know where they are going, because parallels never meet and so never indicate their objective at either end. We shall be obliged to continue examining the varieties of foulness to see which can be charged to the author and which to others. Always we come back to the individual case, as always we must. For we form classifications out of individual cases, not individual cases out of classifications. Classifications are only probabilities deduced from past experience. Our present classifications according to act and scene division show no particular correlation with foulness, and are not likely to be particularly helpful positively on that or most other fundamental problems. They show simply that the way is still wide open for the same kind of fundamental attack that scholars have always used, when they have not become entangled in unproved generalizations.

Each of us would like, of course, to examine critically in minutest detail the fairest of Shakspere's unblotted manuscripts known to Heminges and Cundall. Most of us would rejoice to see even a foul copy, though it were as blotted as Jonson thought it should have been. And having seen we would generously wish to share our treasure trove with others by means of the best collotype reproduction, with Sir Walter Greg checking every detail. Then we would insist that the originals be enshrined in the holy of holies of the British Museum. But the actors and printers of 1621–23 had no such standards of accuracy, no faintest thought that some day such a nemesis would be on the trail of their blissfully ignorant well-doings as Sir Walter Greg; and even if they had, then no inkling of collotype reproduction, no suspicion that out of the fields would one day grow such an unthinkable thing as the British Museum; no veneration for these manuscripts as such—they were not ancient and worm-eaten repositories of Latin and Greek—not even Ben Jonson attempted to preserve the manuscripts of his "Works." But according to the light of their own day these men did very well by their fellow Shakspere, and we should most certainly commend them for having done no worse—and if we are right about the comedies, for not having tried to do any better!

But always in our attempts at vision, the printer, at least, is between us and Shakspere's autograph. The intensive study of

printing for upward of half a century now begins to show what
the printer did, for that exists; but never exactly what he did
it to, for that does not exist, and so far as print is concerned
must remain an inference. At best, the wanted fact can be seen
only behind the veil (of printers' ink) darkly.

And here we sometimes forget that neither a quarto nor
the Folio has any authority in itself. It is the manuscript behind either which has more or less authority according as it
represents Shakespere's original. It is now becoming apparent
that even the printer could have had before him in the majority of cases and perhaps in all only a copy of the sacred
original. Here then again we have also the copyists to "eliminate," even though he be Ralph Crane, evidently faithful in
many things, but as evidently considering many others to be
within his power to shape at will. And the copy a Crane might
have before him to copy was as likely as not to be one already
adapted to some kind of stage purpose, even if it still contained
all the material which had been marked for omission. One may
look at surviving autograph manuscripts of theatrical prove-
nance and shudder or rejoice. Sir Walter Greg has looked un-
flinchingly upon that gorgon in all its nakedness and has not
perished. Evidently there is no royal road directly to Shakspere's unblotted original. Classification of types represented
has its uses, but it throws little light on Shakspere's original. At
best, it is negative, showing that something is wrong, but still
leaving us to infer what is right.

In dealing with manuscripts, one may happily match up his
variants, usually back to two—the hen and the egg. The process
merely uncovers the problem; it does nothing directly to settle
it. But for twenty-two out of thirty-six of Shakspere's plays, we
have only one good text and that printed; in no case any
manuscript at all. We have no ultimate disagreement between
two or more to make it objectively evident that there is error
or change. Even where we have more than one print, we have

a host of contaminating agencies between us and the original
to veto any purely automatic assumption of superiority. In the
individual case, there can be no "better" reading. For any word
in Shakspere anyone can think of a "better" one and many just
as good. With a little prompting from Kellner, he can rewrite
Shakspere many times over, much more to his own liking, else
the fault is his own. To find what could happen does not give
the faintest idea of what did happen. The goodness or the
badness of the individual reading must be determined on its
own. Any existent reading is a good one until it is proved objectively to be bad. For convenience, we may decide upon a
"copy text," or a "substantive text," or a rose by any other
name; but we shall be very unwise if we attribute to that text
any greater authority in the individual case than to any other.
For it is because of our impression from its individual cases
that we have in the first place selected it as our "copy text" or
what not in the second. There is no use trying to lift ourselves
by our bootstraps. An assumption is not a fact.

It is still necessary to use on each individual problem all
the critical resources known, and to hope to discover a few
more. And in doing so, it is notorious that even the worst "bad"
quarto may upon occasion be worth more than all the "good"
texts. The reason is simple; it frequently represents the parent
exemplar at an earlier stage. The problem is to find the cases.
It is to be hoped we shall continue to gather our facts and
attempt to classify them as scholars have always done, but with
perhaps somewhat more circumspect enthusiasm than has sometimes been the case. Each fact must be put into its relative and
relevant background—and that relative and relevant background will be found to be relative and relevant to everything
else in the universe. To be expert in only one technique is to
be fatally ignorant in the whole. Whether we gather pessimisti-
cally or optimistically is a matter of individual taste, just so we
work—blood and sweat, only more abundantly.

Appendix

RIGHTS IN SHAKSPERE'S PLAYS

UPON THE background of the principles we have been examining, it is easily to be demonstrated for Shakspere's plays that the orders of the Lord Chamberlain in 1619 had no effect whatever upon the rights already acquired and confirmed by publication in quarto. First is the fact that in the entry of November 8, 1623, for the First Folio, every previous quarto, good or bad, to the number of twenty plays out of thirty-six is recognized as valid for purposes of license, even though some cases required a great deal of "stretching."

8° Nouembris. 1623 . . .

M^r. Blounte   Isaak Iaggard. Entred for their Copie vnder the hands of M^r. Do^r. Worrall and M^r. Cole warden M^r. William Shakspeers Comedyes Histories, & Tragedyes soe manie of the said Copies as are not formerly entred to other men. vizt. vij^s

Comedyes.	*Histories*
The Tempest	The thirde parte of Henry y^e
The two gentlemen of Verona	sixt
Measure for Measure	Henry the eight
The Comedy of Errors	*Tragedies.*
As you like it	Coriolanus
All's well that ends well	Timon of Athens
Twelfe night	Iulius Caesar
The winters tale	Mackbeth
	Anthonie & Cleopatra
	Cymbeline

[The sum "vij^s" is added in a different ink. It should normally have been 8*s.*][1]

---

1 Greg, *Bibliography,* I, 33. One suspects that the two "Histories" were overlooked in the count.

The title in the entry is that of the First Folio, and the order of mention for the individual plays follows the "Catalogve" in that volume, showing that the order of plays had been determined; but spellings, capitalizations, etc. are different, so that it is not certain that the clerk was following an already printed copy which had been used for checking the licensed and the unlicensed plays.

Two authorities are represented in this entry. "M^r. Do^r. Worrall," as the representative of the Bishop of London (and the Archbishop of Canterbury), passes the volume for inoffensive content. "M^r. Cole warden," as the representative of the Stationers' Company, passes for regularity of entry. Regularity would include the license, for which Worrall is given as authority, and the assurance that these plays were not being published without the consent of the King's men.

Not only are the quarto rights accepted officially here as sufficient for the purpose of license (for publication if for nothing else), but they continue to be valid after the publication of the First Folio in 1623. In contra-distinction, the entry of the previously unentered plays for the First Folio was never used for the publication of a quarto. Of the plays first entered November 8, 1623, only *Julius Caesar,* 1684ff was printed outside the folios during the seventeenth century. For this publication in quarto, there was a separate entry S.R. January 12, 1684, by H. Herringman and R. Everingham. Though Herringman had acquired rights in the folios, nevertheless, for whatever reason, a separate entry was required for publication in quarto. The basic fact is that in the only known instance, publication in quarto required a separate license for the purpose, even for one who had rights in the folios.

But it is equally clear that the entry of 1623 did not in any way affect the rights of those who had already published in quarto. There was a transfer entered S.R. August 4, 1626, from the widow of T. Pavier to E. Brewster and R. Birde of "M^r. Paviers right in Shakesperes plaies or any of them," naming incidentally "The history of Hen: the fift, and the play of the same," and "Tytus & Andronicus." Thus *Henry V* is alluded to in order to distinguish it from the "history of Hen: the fift," and the same reason may lie behind the mention of *Titus.* Then November 8, 1630, there is a transfer from R. Bird to R. Cotes of his right in "Henrye the fift" and "Titus and Andronicus." Besides the two plays mentioned, Pavier's "right in Shakesperes plaies" in 1626 is assumed also to have covered *2 Henry VI* and *3 Henry VI,* confirmed by the transfer in 1630 of "Yorke and Lancaster." But no quarto survives after the First Folio for any of these plays from Pavier's rights. Nevertheless, they were still considered valid within the trade.

For *2 Henry IV, Much Ado, Midsummer-Night's Dream,* and *Troilus,* there were neither quartos nor transfers after 1623. Even before, only *Midsummer-Night's Dream* had been reprinted, and that among the false quartos of 1619. For *Antony and Cleopatra,* there had been no known quarto upon the license of 1608; the play was re-licensed for the First Folio, and there was no quarto thereafter.

John Norton printed *Richard III* in 1629, *1 Henry IV* in 1632, and *Richard II* in 1634. All these had been entered to A. Wise, and transfer was recorded S. R. to M. Law June 25, 1603. Norton had evidently succeeded to Law's right, and there is no record that either Law or Norton had any connection with the First Folio. Wise had entered also *2 Henry IV* and *Much Ado About Nothing* in conjunction with John Aspley, and since Wise did not transfer these, the reasonable assumption is that they remained with Aspley, though there is no record either that Aspley passed his rights or published a quarto. Aspley was later to participate in publishing the First Folio.

On November 19, 1607, transfer was recorderd S.R. from Ling to Smethwick of *Hamlet, A Shrewe, Romeo,* and *Love's Labor's Lost.* Smethwick had editions of *The Shrew* (text of F1) in 1631, and of *Romeo* (undated edition also), and *Hamlet* in 1637. Smethwick belonged to the syndicate for the First Folio, and so apparently felt free to help himself from its text, but he did not publish in right of his connection with the folios. Smethwick's texts were sadly in need of help, for all his previous quartos had "problems" attached to them. If the players had anything to do with "selecting" Smethwick and Aspley, they certainly did not select them for the purity of their quarto texts. But while Smethwick republished his quartos later, helping himself upon occasion to the folio text, yet he published no other plays from the collection than his own.

Four others of the plays belonged singly to individuals, not in the syndicate either; but these plays also followed the usual process. *Merry Wives* (folio text), 1630; *Othello,* 1630; *Merchant of Venice,* 1637; trace their right to the original entries. *Lear,* 1655, traces its right through *Leir.* In some instances, there were further quartos and further transfers in proper succession, but these are not needed to establish the present point.

It is completely clear, not only that the entry for the First Folio

recognized the rights of the previous quartos, but also that publication
of the First Folio in no way affected the rights to the individual plays
which had been printed previously in quarto, whether good or "bad." In
the cases of *Merry Wives* and *The Shrew* (complete substitution of play
for play), even the good text of F1 was substituted for the bad, while
Love's Labor's Lost substituted the better text of F1. *Othello* is suspected
of bettering itself with the aid of F1, and *Richard II* by F2. Decidedly,
the successors to the original owners of the individual plays did not consider that they had given up any right for continued publication, and
there is no record that anyone disagreed.

In view of the fact that the license of 1623 was for the folio collection only, and gave no right to publication of individual plays (at least
none that was exercised in the seventeenth century), and in view of the
fact that the rights of those who had previously published individual plays
were in no way affected, it is clear that the entry S.R. was only of the
First Folio collection as a collection. That evident fact thus raises the
further question of whether the owners of individual plays had been, or
needed to be, in any way consulted about the copy for F1, as is regularly
assumed.[2] Certainly, there is no evidence that any one of them was
consulted, very peculiar in view of the elaborate "arrangements" and
wide-spread sharp practice which is assumed. Surely we need to clear the
evolving legitimacies of the time, instead of interpreting anachronistically
in terms of our prevailing prejudices. Certainly, the players claim they
are using their own complete copies, not anyone's previous copy. Certainly,
they did use their own manuscripts, though they are supposed to have used
also some of the good quartos as agents of transmission, a perfectly
legitimate process.

Following long precedent, the Lord Chamberlain had assumed in
1619 that His Majesty's Players owned their plays absolutely, and had
the right to prevent anyone from printing them without their permission,
if they could enforce the right. The Stationers' Company accepted and
entered for the guidance of the brethren the Lord Chamberlain's order.
On the same assumption, the players themselves came to terms unknown
with publishers and a printer, without causal relationship to previous
publishers or printers in quarto, and proceeded to publication of the First
Folio. In the name of the author, the players asserted their complete
independence of previous publications. They asserted that they owned
and had used the true complete original manuscripts. If they or Shakspere

2 For a cautious and careful summary on this assumption, see Chambers,

had not parted with the rights in these (and there is no single record that they had), then who could have had a right that would stand against theirs, especially since these were now the complete collected works, not a few separate plays, wholly unauthorized by the players who actually owned them? Besides, who was going to "buck" the Lord Chamberlain?

Probably our chief difficulty here has been created by our anachronistic assumptions as to copyright. The term itself did not then exist, and to use it in the modern sense is to beg the question. At that time there was only the right in copy, and we are trying to find out exactly what in 1623 this right was supposed to be for Shakspere's "Works." Entry S.R. gave no one anything—except the clerk his fee. By entry one simply declared to the brethren only that to the best of his belief and opinion he had the right in whole or in part, as stated, in that particular copy as against all brethren. And, for the plays of the King's men at least, by 1623 the officials of the company were supposed to have assured themselves reasonably of these facts before they authorized entry. The Stationers' Company, at least in that day, could not give "copyright"; it could only register right in copy, where it was reasonably assured, and could regulate and adjudicate only between brethren when differences arose. Over the property rights of others the Stationers' Company had no jurisdiction. And outsiders, as such, had no way of defending themselves within the Stationers' Company. Hence the outside interference of the Lord Chamberlain, not theirs, when the rights of the actors were being infringed. The Stationers' Company was now to be certain the property rights of the actors were being properly observed by members. Surely for their own property the actors did not need to consult those who had published without their authorization, especially since they were using their own manuscripts, not reprinting these unauthorized publications. They were in no way infringing upon previous copy for individual plays, but were publishing the whole from the authentic copies.

Symptomatic of the complete independence from the past of this enterprise of the First Folio is the makeup of the "syndicate" which published it. Only two of the group could have had any rights to any of the previous quartos. Smethwick claimed four plays as his in quarto form, and Aspley probably claimed two, their possible total being six out of twenty, as accepted by officials of the Stationers' Company. There is no evidence that the owners of the other fourteen quarto rights were in any way approached. Pavier could claim three, possibly four, as many

William Shakespeare, I, 139 ff.

as Smethwick; and in 1619 he had shown the desire to publish. Law (Norton) could claim three to Aspley's possible two. But Pavier was decidedly out of favor. Why Law's interests were not brought into the deal does not appear. Add that Jaggard and Blount had no quarto rights, and it will be completely clear that this was not a move on the part of quarto owners to unite in producing a complete collection. Pavier's earliest move may have been such, but the actors denigrate the results of it, and claim that they are producing the only true and genuine.

Thus William Jaggard (though dead), Blount, Aspley, and Smethwick are listed in the colophon as having borne the charges of the publication, while on the title-page Isaac Jaggard and Blount, who had entered the new plays, are said to be the "printers." What the agreement of the syndicate was we do not know. Nor do we know except by possible inference whether the "players," the "printers," or the "publishers" took the lead in the enterprise. But the "players" take credit for the publication, and their action in 1619 had occasioned it, while the "printers" and the "publishers" are not given a word to say. No doubt they were quite content to take the cash and let the credit go.

If, as they claim, the players took the lead in publication, then they probably turned to Aspley and Smethwick as previously interested publishers, against whom apparently they had no grudge, not to Pavier, of course. These publishers would doubtless have suggested the firm of Jaggard, with the backing of Blount, for the job. No blame would attach to William Jaggard for his share in the Pavier deal, since he was merely the hired printer, and presumably printed only what was set before him, "as per contract." No doubt Pavier had shown good judgment in his selection of a printer. But William Jaggard's son Isaac survived to get his name upon the title-page in 1623, after the death of his father. Thus only two of the numerous former publishers of Shakspere's plays are represented in the First Folio. From every point of view, the First Folio was treated as a "new deal."

No doubt, "Mr. Cole warden" had done his duty and had found that no one had a valid counterclaim to Shakspere's "Works." One phase of that duty was to be certain that these plays had been properly licensed as fit for consumption, and "Mr. Dor. Worrall" is recorded as having satisfied this regulation. This raises the question of when and how the good Doctor had proceeded. Did he himself read every manuscript of every play in the exact copy submitted to the printer? Theoretically, that

was true for every publication. If he did so, did he read the whole at
one time, or did he pass play by play as each was about to be submitted
to the printer? Did he simply accept the previously printed plays on
assurance that no offensive matter would be added or continued, and then
confine his attentions to the previously unprinted plays, for which he is
made specifically responsible in the S.R. entry? Or did he simply accept
on assurance the copy of each play which bore the license of the Master
of the Revels?

Perhaps this sample of questions, for there are many more, is
sufficient to show the reader something of what we need to know, and
probably can never know fully, in order to interpret the role of the censor
in the plays of the First Folio. We may be certain that the Master of the
Revels had operated before the play was staged, and Sir George Buck,
Master of the Revels, had taken the place of the Bishop's official by
1607 for licensing plays for print, except when he was not available. On
such occasions, Buck's deputy, or a designated deputy of the Bishop's
office might serve. So far as I know, we have no actual instance; but with
Buck and his deputy, one is entitled to suspect that, having read for the
stage, the rereading for print was at most perfunctory. And one suspects
that under the circumstances Taverner of the Bishop's office was not
unduly particular to check upon the previous checking of the Master of
the Revels in licensing the play.

But neither Buck nor Taverner was overtly concerned in the official
licensing of these plays for the First Folio. The last entry S.R. for Sir
George Buck was February 22, 1622. The last time Taverner, as Bishop's
licenser, substituted for Buck was January 15, 1620. Then January 20,
1623, Sir John Ashley appears (this entry as the first being celebrated by
the clerk with the wrong title for him, which he amended). Then Sir
Henry Herbert appeared March 12, 1624. All individual plays had been
passed by the Master of the Revels, as usual. Only on the First Folio
does the Bishop's official function, a doctor at that, "M^r. Do^r. Worrall."
But Worrall was a regular licenser for George Montaigne, who became
Bishop of London July 20, 1621, and was translated in 1627. So "master
Worrall"[3] appears first as licenser November 16, 1621, licensing some
sixty-odd items by September 15, 1623. Then his Oxford D.D. of 1623
(incorporated at Cambridge 1624; see Venn) took effect to make him
"Master Doctor Worrall" in an entry of September 27, 1623, and in

---

3 *Transcript,* ed. Arber, IV. 62, p. 24.

numerous others thereafter to October 4, 1628.[4] So "Master Doctor Worrall" was a veteran licenser, though the First Folio was only his fourth appearance as "Doctor."

The First Folio thus received the routine treatment of a book, not that of a play; but this fact answers none of the questions we raised above concerning the method of censorship. Rather, it brings in an unknown quantity. How seriously was the good Doctor likely to take his function? This might give some guess as to how carefully and when he performed it. But so far the Doctor, as censor, appears to be a completely unknown quantity.

4 *Transcript,* ed. Arber, IV. 203, p. 169.

INDEXES

The following indexes are divided into three separate categories, as follows

I. Index to Bibliographical References

II. Analytical Index on Acts and Scenes

III. General Index